T0303599

PENGUIN BOOKS
THE GLOBAL CITIZEN

Patrick Tsang is the Chairman of Tsangs Group and the Hong Kong Ambassadors Club ('HKAC'). Tsangs Group is an innovation-focused family office that bridges East and West with the mission to invest in global opportunities in technology which create a positive impact to make our world a better place.

Patrick is a graduate of the College of Law in England, and a qualified solicitor in Hong Kong, England, and Wales. As a philanthropic advocate, he is the past president of the Rotary E-Club of Hong Kong and has supported charities across Asia and the UK. Currently, Patrick is studying at the Owner/President Management Program (OPM) at Harvard Business School. He is a member of the Monaco Private Label Young Leaders and the Global One Chapter YPO (Young Presidents' Organisation). Notable acknowledgments include being awarded the China Economic Person of the Year during the China Economic Development Forum in 2014. He is also an international keynote speaker on finance and investment, technology, and leadership.

Patrick's life motto is 'anything is possible', the same title as his podcast series featuring some of the most influential people worldwide, who generously share their insights on their road to success. The mission is to share positivity, overcome challenges, and create One World together.

ADVANCE PRAISE FOR *THE GLOBAL CITIZEN*

'Patrick is someone whose drive and commitment to success in business is equaled by his passion for life. His experiences around the world have given him a unique perspective that has made him a new breed of Global Citizen, equally at home in Asia, the Middle East, and the West and this dynamic has enabled him to spot opportunities others may miss.'

—HH Prince Bandar Bin Saud Bin Khalid Al Saud,
secretary general, King Faisal Foundation (KFF)
and Chairman of the Board of Directors of
Al Khozama Investment Company

'Patrick has extensive experience in business, and has foresight to expand into emerging markets and seek new opportunities. In this book, he shares his real-world experience and business philosophy with candid insights, making it an invaluable resource for anyone seeking guidance.'

—The Honourable Jeffrey Lam, GBM, GBS, JP,
Member of the Executive Council and Legislative
Council of Hong Kong SAR Government

'I have known Patrick for many years, and he is not only a global business leader but he is also a true and kind gentleman that I respect and have the privilege to call my friend.'

—Jean-Claude Van Damme, martial artist and actor

'The world is global whether weak isolationist politicians like it or not, and Patrick Tsang gives us a world view to bring people closer together for a more healthy and prosperous world. Read it and learn how to reach across cultures for everyone's benefit.'

—Tim Draper, Silicon Valley venture capitalist,
the founding partner of Draper Associates

'Patrick is a visionary leader and cultural bridge-builder, weaving together different cultures for a brighter, more interconnected future.'

—Anthony Scaramucci, former
White House communications director,
founder and managing partner of Skybridge Capital,
and founder and chairman of SALT

'Patrick Tsang is a magnetic leader; he draws many different kinds of people to him. He is constantly curious, which means his broad network gives him a refreshing perspective on the world, life, and business.'

—Caroline Rush CBE, CEO, British Fashion Council

'Patrick has a genuine desire to uplift those around him. With his compassionate spirit he not only inspires young leaders but also serves as a catalyst for unity and positive change.'

—John Barnes MBE, England and
Liverpool football player

'Patrick is one of the most genuine people you'll ever meet, and it's clear that kindness forms the basis of his success. Whether it's personal or business matters you might be dealing with, you can be sure he will help lift you up!'

—Sue Pickford Cheung,
award-winning author of *Chinglish*

'Patrick is a true leader who walks his talk.'

—Preston Smiles, author, speaker, and entrepreneur

'Patrick Tsang is a leader in the world of international investment and business who brings expertise, passion, and humanity to all his endeavors. More importantly, he is a true global citizen who

has both inspired and supported me and many others over the years. I'm grateful to count him as a mentor and friend.'
—Courtney Fingar, founder, Foreign Direct
Investment journalist and commentator

'Patrick Tsang's *The Global Citizen* is a testament to the power of courage and resilience. Through his family's remarkable journey from China to the UK, Tsang's narrative inspires readers to embrace change and pursue their dreams with unwavering determination—an entrepreneurial spirit that transcend borders and generations. The book is a captivating blend of personal history and universal lessons, *The Global Citizen* reminds us that greatness awaits those who dare to step outside their comfort zones.'
—Claire Chang, founding partner, igniteXL Ventures

'If you've ever been curious about how to foster deeper business connections, work effectively across borders, and make a positive global impact, *The Global Citizen* will teach you how to navigate the business landscape with ease and confidence.'
—Jessica Chen, Emmy-Award winner,
founder and CEO of Soulcast Media,
author of *Smart, Not Loud*

The Global Citizen
Building Bridges from East to West in Business

Patrick Tsang

PENGUIN BOOKS

An imprint of Penguin Random House

PENGUIN BOOKS

Penguin Books is an imprint of the Penguin Random House group of
companies whose addresses can be found at
global.penguinrandomhouse.com

Published by Penguin Random House SEA Pte Ltd
40 Penjuru Lane, #03-12, Block 2
Singapore 609216

First published in Penguin Books by Penguin Random House SEA 2024

ISBN 9789815204766

Typeset in Garamond by MAP Systems, Bengaluru, India
Printed at Markono Print Media Pte Ltd, Singapore

www.penguin.sg

Contents

Part III: Self-Improvement

Foreword

With great enthusiasm, I write this foreword for *The Global Citizen*, written by my good friend and business partner, Patrick Tsang. As I read the personal anecdotes of Patrick in this book, I thoroughly enjoyed reading the story of his grandfather's journey in the 1950s from Hong Kong to Liverpool, creating a universal bridge through food and culture. It is evident that the spark he had to leave Asia and set up in an unknown country is the same drive and mindset that Patrick holds, which led him to revolutionize the family business.

My name is John Textor, and I am an American businessman focusing on technology. I have known Patrick for many years. We got to know each other when I founded Pulse Evolution, which produced digital humans. I created the Tupac and Michael Jackson holograms, and Patrick was instrumental in helping me with capital and making the company grow and evolve. Eventually, we merged with FuboTV and took the company public on the New York Stock Exchange.

We flew for business on many trips to London, New York, Hong Kong, and Tokyo, got to know each other, and became very good friends. He even visited me in my Bahamas home during COVID-19 so he could get his fourteen-day requirement before going to his Harvard Business School course!

Now, we are joining forces again to look at sports, media, and entertainment opportunities. Our business partnership has always been a success; our friendship has gone from strength to strength.

My latest venture is in football, and we now own four clubs in England, France, Brazil, and Belgium. One needs a global vision to succeed and understand all the different cultures involved.

He is a global citizen who blends East and West, which helps him in his investment business. He is grounded and responsible and will do anything to help others and someone to rely on. His life motto is 'anything is possible', and his positivity makes you want to work with him.

If you want to learn and pick up something interesting, no matter who you are and what background, you will learn something from this book and enjoy yourself reading through the stories that take you to all corners of the world, including to the top of Mount Kenya with Sir Richard Branson.

Introduction

We have all heard the phrase, 'The sky's the limit.' I've always been a smart-ass—or tried to be! I always ask, 'Why is that when there is outer space? The sky is not the limit, there is no limit.' Why should our abilities and ambitions, like the sky, be limited? Limits exist only in the confines of the mind. For me, the sky was just the beginning.

I grew up in the sky—the Blue Sky (more on this later), to be specific—and spent the next few decades building bridges back down to Earth. It was not obvious to me at the time, but no matter where I was or what I was doing, I was always building bridges, one step at a time, to get to the next destination for myself. Eventually, it became bigger than just me, I found myself building bridges to connect people, businesses, and cultures from all over the world.

I began my life as an average child of immigrants, who listened religiously to his loving but strict parents and was obsessed with Bruce Lee. I was very diligent when I was expected to be, particularly when it came to schoolwork and working at my family's restaurant. In spite of this, I was also somewhat aimless, floundering in the current created by my family. I always had high expectations of myself, but what I wanted to do, I did not really have a clue when I was younger. It was only after years of academic trials, university, law school, becoming a lawyer and a financier, and entering the business world that I was able to break free from the script given to me at birth. As the chairman of

Tsangs Group, a global family office that seeks to bridge East and West through astute and future-focused investments, I have become an advocate of technology, innovation, and progress.

Today, I am an investor and a financier. As an IPO and M&A professional, I have participated in a significant number of transactions globally. I am a qualified solicitor in the UK, Wales, and Hong Kong, and I am actively involved in a variety of charitable and business organizations worldwide. In 2014, I was awarded the China Economic Person of the Year award at the China Economic Forum. I was a Fellow of the Duke of Edinburgh's International Award World Fellowship in the UK. The Duke of Edinburgh's International Award is a program that was founded by the late Prince Philip, Duke of Edinburgh, in 1956. It is a self-development program for young people aged fourteen to twenty-four and operates in over 140 countries around the world. The International Award World Fellowship is a group of individuals who are committed to supporting the aims and objectives of the award program. The fellowship works to promote the program and to provide support and guidance to those involved in delivering the award to young people.

I have invested in exciting ventures in space, biotech, renewables, gaming and entertainment technology, movies, AI, robotics, fintech, and blockchain. These are areas I never imagined I would have the opportunity to work in, or interact with, on such a personal level. All of this may seem impressive or even impossible. You might assume I received all the rewards of success on a silver platter, but I can assure you that my journey was anything but easy. There is no such thing as an easy life. Bruce Lee says, 'Never pray for an easy life but for the strength to endure a difficult one.' I never thought it would be easy. Indeed, I would not have wanted the process to be easy. My journey was not even headed in the right direction at the beginning. At every point, I improvised and did what was necessary without much planning.

In the course of my journey, I learned a lot and made a lot of corrections. After listening to my family for so long, I eventually had come to accept and appreciate their advice, and later, I had to learn to unlearn certain things. Throughout my life, I have had to learn how to listen to myself, to my instincts and heart. I have to digest and make my own decisions, to make my own mistakes, and to find my own way. To build a bridge between the viewpoints of my family and mine, I had to learn to listen to others, but more importantly, myself. It was more difficult than it sounded, as elders, teachers, and mentors are highly respected in Asian culture. The majority of my youth was spent oscillating between total obedience and wanton rebellion before finding a respectable middle ground. It created conflict, which was difficult when I was young. I feel, however, that having grown up in two different cultures has given me the best of both worlds, allowing me to see the world in a very different and unique manner.

The ultimate lesson: we should respect and listen to elders, but we must digest the information ourselves and, ultimately, make our own decisions. We must live our own lives instead of someone else's. Balance is critical in life; until we die, we must maintain an equilibrium that works for our individual lives.

In the end, it may sound simple, but it has been a long and arduous journey to attain that wisdom. I had to unlearn Asian conditioning and resist the temptation to go in the opposite direction. I concluded that there is no right or wrong in life, and that all cultures are slightly different. In spite of this, we are all human beings and very similar in most aspects, and we all have lessons to learn from one another. In order to benefit from any culture, we must retain its essential lessons and discard its useless ones. As always, it is a matter of perspective.

Through the years, I have mastered the art of incorporating the most effective elements of each culture into my arsenal. Building bridges at home was only the beginning of my journey.

My destiny was to build bridges between the East and the West. My mission would be to bridge the various cultures that shape the landscape of our world. I became the Eastern expert for Western companies and the Western expert for Eastern companies.

As a result, I am a mixture of cultures. With Tsangs Group, I have become a global citizen, which helps with the business and its growth, and I am proud that it has followed me cross the bridge to success on the international stage.

There have been many setbacks and mistakes, but there have also been moments of clarity and epiphany. Over the years, I have been building integrity, striving for improvement, and developing empathy to become the leader I am today, a leader of a group of like-minded success stories—and I am far from finished. One of my dreams is to harness the power of social media and explore the potential of transformative technologies like space travel.

Looking back, I am pleased with the journey I have undertaken, the bridges I have built, and the success I have achieved. Thanks to the people who helped me along the way—including family, friends, colleagues, partners, and mentors. My memories are infused with pride and gratitude.

Although I am thrilled to see how far I have come, I am not surprised by the progress I have made. While it may sound arrogant, I was always confident in my abilities, and this coupled with discipline, consistency, and dedication lead to my success. According to Henry Ford, 'Whether you think you can or cannot—you are right.'

There is only one motto that I follow: 'Anything is possible.' No matter where you come from, you can achieve anything if you have the determination, grit, and time. There is no limit to how far you can soar, far beyond anything you could have ever imagined, including your own expectations. You are capable of beating the odds, obtaining degrees, starting a business, and shattering glass ceilings. There is no limit to what is possible, because, literally, anything is possible. Do not be deceived by anyone, especially your greatest enemy: yourself.

Why I Wrote This Book

In spite of the fact that 'anything is possible', I have observed that many people make fatal mistakes when they attempt to achieve their dreams. There is no doubt that everyone makes mistakes in business and in life, but I am not referring to an ill-advised business venture or an awkward client meeting. No, what I'm talking about are fundamental misunderstandings of mindset and belief that can cause your journey to end before it has even begun. I've seen many people become discouraged because of where they come from. They believe that they will never rise beyond the level at which they were born. In the past, I have observed friends who had admirable intentions lose their way because they listened to the wrong mentors and ignored the right ones. Investors and colleagues have failed to trust themselves and lost everything as a result. Although these qualities are invisible and may seem unimportant to someone more concerned with numbers than with what is going on inside, trust me, they are more critical than anything else. It is possible to save a bad quarter with a few good deals. However, the problem of a lack of integrity is not easily rectified.

The purpose of this book is to provide leadership advice to future and current leaders. I share my experiences in the hope to inspire innovators, partners, and investors who believe in my vision of globalization and advancement.

I see globalization as the interconnection of people and situations influenced by technological advancements in the last twenty to thirty years. While this has brought people closer through tools like smartphones and international travel, it has also affected social interaction skills. However, I do believe that recent geopolitical shifts towards polarization and nationalism challenge the collaborative spirit of globalization. I support globalization in both business and investment, emphasizing its positive impact when executed with the right intentions and strategies as it serves a greater purpose.

Although anyone can achieve success, it does not mean that everyone will succeed. The road to success takes more than a dream and disciplined work. I would like to share with you some of the methods I discovered while climbing to the top. My goal is to share my experience and expertise with the next generation of young leaders. This will enable them to build bridges between where they came from and where they are heading. I would then like to demonstrate how to cross that bridge—balanced and supported—into this promised land.

This book is organized into three pillars, each integral to one's metamorphosis into a world-class business leader. They are simple but far from easy to accomplish:

1. Integrity
2. Empathy
3. Self-Improvement

Moreover, each pillar is further divided into chapters, each of which will impart a valuable lesson in self-improvement and business acumen. It is my intention to share with you the story of my life to date, from my humble beginnings as a victim of bullying and family pressure, through my winding career path across the globe to my present-day endeavours. Here, I will share how I transformed my differences from lead weights to gold wings by finding my inner voice.

There are many benefits to reading this book, both in business and in your personal life. You can achieve what I did without experiencing the pain of learning everything the hard way. Rather than suffering through the storm, I wish to help you see the silver linings.

This book may not be suitable for those who prefer to stay within their familiar habits and are not looking to challenge themselves or strive for growth. It is geared towards individuals who are motivated to pursue their goals and are willing to put in the effort to achieve them, rather than taking the easiest route.

If you wish to learn how to play the cards you are dealt to win any game you play and overcome any challenge the world brings your way, this book is for you.

If you want to learn how to break the mould while benefiting from the wisdom of tradition, this book is for you.

If you are a current or future leader who wishes for nothing more than to touch the sky and beyond, this book is for you.

If you have been trying to get your feet off the ground for years, I dream this book will give you wings.

Without further ado, let's start from where it all began . . . a clear blue sky.

Part I

Integrity

1

Fortune Favours the Bold

My family comes from a long line of farmers, part of an ethnic group called the Hakka. Originally a nomadic tribe, the Hakka moved throughout China and were never considered locals wherever they went. As a matter of fact, Hakka 客家 is a Chinese word that translates to 'guest people/family'.

My family's nomadic past ended approximately 700 years ago when they migrated from Guangdong (Canton) province in Southern China to Hong Kong. Hakkas are originally from Henan province, but many Hakkas migrated to the southern parts of the country. We trace our ancestry to Shandong province, which is the northern province where Tsingtao beer originated! The Tsang family's connections to our Hong Kong village now goes back fourteen generations.

My great-grandfather was born in 1898, in Hong Kong, and grew up during the Qing dynasty. In addition to his distinctive Qing pigtail, he had four wives and very limited resources. Like the generations before him, he was an illiterate farmer toiling away in the tropical heat of southern China.

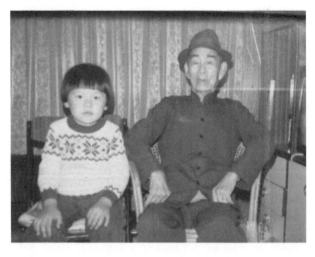

*Patrick as a young boy with his great-grandfather, Tsang Man Cheong,
at their old family home in Sha Tau Kok, Hong Kong, when the
family moved away from the village (circa 1980)*

While he was a simple man in many respects, he believed that true power came from the pen, not the sword. As a result, he decided to use every ounce of energy, will, and savings to educate his family. It was his decision to educate his eldest son—the only son of the first wife—my grandfather, which changed the course of the history of our family.

My grandfather was only educated for three years, from the age of eight to the age of eleven. In spite of this, he was able to learn to read and write in that short period of time. As was common for poor families at the time, he began working at the age of six. Most importantly, he left the village in his teens to seek better employment and learned a bit of English as he went. Even though his skills were rough and weak, they were sufficient to carry him to a new world. During the early 1950s, he made a fateful decision, leaving his 700-year-old roots in Hong Kong to start over in Liverpool, UK.

A Norwegian ship called the *Blue Funnel* brought my grandfather and eleven other Hong Kong Chinese to Liverpool in 1956. It took two months to complete the trip, which included stops in Singapore, Sri Lanka, various parts of Africa, and the Suez Canal.

The first leg of the trip consisted of a seven-day journey from Hong Kong to Singapore. The ship served only Western food on board, which was unfamiliar to the Chinese passengers. Their diets consisted of rice, vegetables, and, when it was available, a small amount of meat.

Upon landing in Singapore, these young Chinese men (all around twenty years old) rushed off the boat and headed directly to Chinatown with only one goal in mind: to stuff their faces with the most delicious traditional Chinese food.

It was one of the finest meals they had eaten in a long time. As my grandfather looked up after a satisfying meal, he noticed that the restaurant was named Blue Sky. At that moment, he made a promise to himself that one day he would open a restaurant called Blue Sky, no matter what it took. He was twenty-seven years old when he arrived in the UK and began his strange new life. Despite his limited knowledge of English, he began his new journey into the unknown with no idea of when he will return, if ever, and with the determination to survive in a world very different from the one he had left behind.

When the boat landed, someone from the local Chinese consulate was waiting at the front of the boat and asked the Chinese contingent if anyone spoke English. He was the only person with any knowledge of English, so he raised his hand to speak.

He was offered a position immediately in one of the first Chinese restaurants in the UK. As the only Chinese employee who spoke some English, he received generous tips from the clientele, which he used to support the family back home.

After working as a waiter for two to three years, he was able to save enough money to start the restaurant that he had always dreamed of, ever since that fateful meal in Singapore. His first restaurant, named Blue Sky, was opened in Southport, in the northwest of England, with a small loan from his boss (a practice he continued with his own staff in the future).

Like the Blue Sky restaurant in Singapore a few years earlier, this restaurant served as a small portal back home for my grandfather and others who missed traditional cuisine.

From the beginning, Blue Sky was a success. It was one of the first Chinese restaurants in the UK, which was still considered exotic and risky at the time. Despite the fact that the venture could have been a failure, my grandfather was savvy in his approach. Having designed the menu to suit Western palates, even the most wary of customers began arriving to try this new exotic menu—and they were not disappointed. My grandfather's restaurant became a favourite destination for celebrities and prominent figures in the area, and he achieved an unprecedented level of success.

Using his knowledge of UK customs and knowledge of life back home, he created a restaurant experience that made his customers feel welcome and excited about trying something new. The quality had to always be up there so they would keep coming back for more!

You must be the first, the best, or the most different in order to succeed in business. Having incorporated pieces of all three tenets into his restaurant from the outset, my grandfather was one of the first to do so, and his ability to bridge Western customs with Eastern delicacies made him unique. Although I may be biased, I believe that he was a pioneer in the field.

Food has always been a unifying force in families, especially in Asian cultures. And our family was no exception. That is how they demonstrate their love and affection for one another. Among Chinese people, it is much more common to say, 'Have you eaten?' than 'How are you?' to family and friends, which further emphasizes the cultural significance of food.

The Hakka are a group of people who are not united by religion or geography. If one wishes to find the connecting thread, one must examine the community more closely. At a time when most people worked in hot, humid rice fields, luxuries and pleasures were few and far between. A robust culinary culture emerged among the Hakka as food became the most accessible pleasure for the common person. Food plays a significant role not only in the culture of my people, but also in my own identity.

Since my childhood, my parents and grandparents have never said, 'I love you.' Instead, they came from a culture in which love was demonstrated rather than spoken. There was still a collective memory of deprivation from long ago, and the ability to provide three delicious meals each day was the ultimate expression of love.

Food is the reason why Tsangs Group exists, not only because it gave my family a foundation in the West. As a child, I spent weekends working in those hot, busy kitchens with my parents. Unlike my siblings, I spent more time moving from fryer to fryer preparing Westernized versions of Chinese food that would not be recognized on the streets of Hong Kong or Beijing. My early years were defined by a perfect synthesis of food, family, and culture.

Having done my part for the family and pleasing my parents, who appreciated cheap child labour, I established a strong work ethic and gained a solid understanding of business principles.

My grandfather's success was not limited to his food, however. Throughout the years, his business skills developed, and he soon flourished. Eventually, he built an empire of over thirty to forty successful restaurants in the northwest of England—Liverpool, Manchester, Blackpool, etc. In spite of this, he never forgot where he came from or his father's faith in him as a beacon of hope for his community.

Most of his income was sent home to Hong Kong, to his father, his four wives, and many children, as well as to his own wife and children. With the income my grandfather derived from the restaurants, he was able to assist not only his family but also the 300 families in his village back home to relocate to UK. Consequently, each family became a business owner, opening Chinese restaurants that contributed to the British economy. As the '60s and '70s progressed, Chinese restaurants became the hottest place to go for a nice evening out.

Although there are Chinese restaurants everywhere today, and most of the second and third generations, including myself, have not continued the restaurant tradition, I have great respect for my grandfather and those who preceded him. In this way, my grandfather was able to give back to both of his homes—his birthplace in the East and his new home in the West.

While my grandfather achieved great success in his restaurant business, he did not intend to stop there. As his culinary success grew, he began parlaying the proceeds into increasingly successful real estate investments from the 1970s through the 1990s. The property market is a common way for Eastern families to grow wealth—once again, he benefited from both his experience in the East and his familiarity with the West in order to increase his success.

Tsangs Group began as a collection of real estate investments, primarily in the UK, Hong Kong, and China. At the outset, there was little strategy involved, other than the fact that real estate was considered to be a good, income-producing investment. The family office grew as property values in Hong Kong and China skyrocketed. The investment focus of Tsangs Group did not expand until I joined the organization, but that is a story for a later time.

In the end, Blue Sky's success was a result of immigrants supporting immigrants. My grandfather opened his first restaurant with the assistance of his employer (who was technically a competitor). After that, he worked to support his employees by assisting them with the opening of their own restaurants. In this way, everyone was able to win.

However, my grandfather came from modest beginnings, and he achieved unparalleled success. His father was unable to afford to send his son to school full time but only for a few years, and that was all my grandfather had at his disposal. He boarded a ship without knowing how the West functioned or differed from the world he knew. It was not his intention to own or operate a business in the UK because he did not have experience. It was not his intention to do any of this; he simply tried his best to make the situation work, and he succeeded.

It was because of his hard work and steadfast determination that he achieved his father's goals and made his family proud— the crowning achievement of Eastern culture. It is in my blood to not fear the future, not give up, and always strive for success. It has been passed down through generations. I was born under a bright blue sky.

Key Takeaway

Fortune really does favour the bold. Do not be afraid to leave your comfort zone, throw caution to the wind, and see what the universe has to offer.

2

Clouds Around a New Blue Sky

1968, my grandfather's restaurant in Blackpool was visited by a police officer from the Royal Ulster Constabulary who was on vacation. The officer commented that it was one of the best meals he had ever had, and he asked my grandfather to consider opening one in Northern Ireland, as they had none at the time. This encounter sparked my grandfather's interest in opening a restaurant there. Soon after, he established New Blue Sky, the first Chinese restaurant in Northern Ireland. This is where my parents' story and the story of my immediate family began.

I grew up in a family-run business, practically living at New Blue Sky. It was one of the largest and best restaurants in Northern Ireland and Ireland at the time, with all employees being either family members or from Lai Chi Wo, our ancestral village in Hong Kong. My grandfather only hired family members, keeping all jobs within the family circle.

From a young age, I helped out at the restaurant and takeaway until I left home for university at eighteen. This is what taught me hard work ethic, grit, and the value of money. Every week I would earn some pocket money from my parents. Being able to earn a few pounds from running around a smoky, oily, and hot kitchen was extremely satisfying. During my time there, I completed a variety of tasks, helping to make some of our well-known dishes like chicken curry, sweet & sour chicken, and fried noodles. I also helped assemble orders, wash dishes, chop vegetables, debone chicken, cook, and more. The atmosphere was always busy and lively, with children and adults running around to complete various tasks. Every day felt like a celebration, like Christmas or Chinese New Year. My grandfather and father were both huge inspirations to me and served as influential mentors during my formative years. I loved working in the restaurant, not for the money or love of the job, but because I got to spend time with my family, be responsible, contribute to the family, and help demonstrate that I was a good, obedient son. Family is intensely important to Eastern cultures, and we were no exception. I was raised to respect my elders and did so without question. My family surrounded me, and I thought the world of them.

My grandfather was a proud, street smart, and clever man. My father, on the other hand, was not as driven as he could have been. My father was brilliant in many ways yet exhibited laziness in everything he did—be it business or personal. I always find that the laziest people are always the smartest. They think of the best ways to do the least. Even though they are smart, they may not end up being the most successful. You may be wondering where I get this logic from. We are naturally inclined towards laziness, seeking efficiency to achieve more with less effort. Many intelligent individuals are inherently lazy, finding the quickest and most effective ways to complete tasks, giving them more time for personal pursuits, though they may not end up being successful.

My mother was kind, caring, selfless, and hardworking; although she tended to stay out of trouble and was sometimes too innocent and risk-averse. We came from a traditional Chinese family, an Asian family where the mother takes care of everything—from shopping to cooking. She patiently made everything happen for us and never complained about how hard she worked and sacrificed, managing the household, and going to work. She just got on with things, a trait which has passed on to me. There is no point complaining about situations, what cards you are dealt, or what you must go through. You have to keep running, improvising, adapting, and doing your best, and you will see results after a long time of discipline, consistency, and hard work.

That is where I get it from; her philosophy is 'actions speak louder than words'. Although she wants me to succeed, she thinks that I am working too hard; her mindset is boxed in, while my father had a more limitless idea of thinking outside the box. I am a combination of laziness and hard work, highlighting the coexistence of these opposing traits. The question stands: Can someone be both lazy and hardworking? I believe so. Lazy individuals often leverage their intelligence to optimize efficiency, doing the least to achieve the most.

Patrick, alongside his parents and siblings Tracy and Ed, captured in Belfast, Ireland, in 1983

Communication was challenging for my parents, especially with their children. We never said, 'I love you', or, 'I miss you', or showed any physical affection, even though we knew deep down that our parents loved us. Instead, my parents provided stability for our family, which was especially valuable in a competitive world where fast food and, later, the internet became prevalent.

Even if mum and dad did not tell us they loved us, we knew they did. There were not many family holidays—the kids were usually packed off to spend time with relatives in Blackpool or Hong Kong—and it was rare to see them at dinner time because they were always working. Still, they offered something magical instead: stability.

Growing up, I faced a number of challenges. Despite having a loving family, I struggled with the fact that I did not speak any English when I started at a Protestant school at the age of four. My mother was young and did not know about the British education system, and as a result, I did not apply for entry into kindergarten or nursery, so I missed out on those early years of education. What we do know now is that it is important for children to learn as much as they can as early as they can, as it helps with their development and attitude toward learning and life.

Before school, I did not interact much with people outside my family, and only spoke Hakka—a dialect of Chinese similar to Cantonese—at home. My grandfather had a basic understanding of English, but my grandmother did not even know how to read or write Chinese and did not speak any English at all. My father's English was better than my grandfather's, but my mother had the best English skills out of all of them.

However, their English was still limited, and they did not know how to teach me English and about life in the UK. They learned very basic English as they lived in the country, more through experience than through formal education. This meant that I felt like I was living in two different worlds at the same time, which was difficult and confusing when I was young, but has ended up being a blessing later in life.

Additionally, I grew up in Belfast during The Troubles, a period of political and sectarian conflict in Northern Ireland. There was a lot of unrest and violence in the city and a constant tension in the air. It was normal for me at the time, but looking back, it was like living in a warzone. For example, when we took the bus to Belfast City Centre, it would stop at checkpoints twice, where armed police would search the bus for suspicious people, materials, or activity. Bombs and bomb scares were a regular occurrence in my early years.

I did not understand the prejudice and banter between Protestants and Catholics when I was younger. To me, they looked and sounded the same and believed in the same God, so I could not understand why they were divided. I ended up joining in with the banter against Catholics to fit in, even though I did not really understand why I was doing it.

I lived in a Protestant area and went to a Protestant school. I did not have any personal animosity toward Catholics, but I did not want to be bullied or seen as different. I am proud to say that I have learned over time that we are all the same, and that our differences do not really matter that much.

Even today, my old school friends joke about Catholics, and I do not understand the hatred behind it. I have learned that these attitudes are often a result of conditioning and propaganda over an extended period of time, and it takes a considerable amount of time to unlearn them. I am grateful to have become a global citizen and tech nomad, which has helped me to see things from a different perspective.

Growing up as Chinese in Belfast had disadvantages, but also had its advantages. We were never caught in the crossfire between Protestants and Catholics, and both groups were friendly with us. Over time, I learned that I could be friends with anyone, regardless of their background. As Bruce Lee said, 'Under the sky, under the heavens, there is but one family.'

When I was twelve, we visited a relative's home and met a neighbour of theirs, a Catholic girl named Laura. We were all playing with a football on the streets and took a liking to each other. I was so excited, but the next day I did not have the courage to tell my school friends, as they were Protestant, and she was Catholic. Nothing would have happened or developed, but looking back, I realize how stupid it was that divisions would affect a Chinese boy to the point of not being able to like a girl because she was Catholic. The ironic thing is, I was not even Protestant or Catholic myself. I do not believe in human-made rules that have no logic.

These rules were set in place to control the masses. I have always been rebellious and curious, and I will never be subject to any rules if I think they are unfair or illogical. I always ask why. I think we all should.

The first day of school remains a vivid memory, one of the most significant experiences in my life. At the age of four, I was seated in a classroom and school environment that was unfamiliar to me. I had never been away from my family and parents before, and I was surrounded by unfamiliar children and an atmosphere that was strange to me. As a person of colour, I had never before been in a room with all white people, and I felt confused, scared, nervous, disoriented, and unsure of what was happening.

During the morning break, all the kids pulled out their packed snacks with milk and biscuits. My mother, who was not familiar with the Western education system, had not packed me anything to eat during break time. Thankfully, a teacher brought me some milk and biscuits, which I was very grateful for, but I was confused about why I did not have the same snacks as everyone else. Was I not good enough?

After lunch, we all went to the playground and began climbing and running, just being kids. I ended up in a little alley at the back of the school. I was crumpled up into a little ball in the corner outside the school canteen. I remember vividly a big tree overlooking the spot, so the alley was very dark. There were leaves from the trees all over the floor, and I can remember the smell and the dampness around me as five boys cornered me and started picking on me. I couldn't understand them or what was happening, but I could tell that their words were not kind.

Before I knew what was happening, they started physically attacking me. I tried to protect myself by rolling into a ball and hiding from their blows. I had never been hit before and experienced physical pain for the first time. It was surreal and terrifying. I eventually ran back to the classroom library and curled up in a corner. I cried nonstop and was extremely scared.

My teacher came to me, and I tried to tell her what was wrong, but I could only do so in Chinese while she tried to comfort me in English. I felt scared, lost, confused, and utterly alone, even though it was a crowded room. The experience left me deeply scarred, and I kept asking myself, 'Why me?'

It was not until much later that I realized the answer to that question: ignorance. They did not know who I was, and I did not know who they were. All they saw was that I looked different, and if the atmosphere we were all growing up in had taught us anything, it was that the 'other' was dangerous. Human beings are fearful of something different. It was easier to attack the other pre-emptively, than be attacked by it. It was a lesson that I carried with me for far too long.

This kind of bullying continued for the first few years at school. I always fought back, sometimes winning, and sometimes losing. I remember always being called names about being Chinese, a 'chinky', and people pulling their eyes. They even went so far to call me a yellow belly. Feelings of anger, frustration, and helplessness were all trapped inside. Sometimes it would erupt, and sometimes, I would hold it in and it would then erupt later.

Over time, I began to realize that the bullying would not stop. From that point on, I always wanted to prove that I had as much value as anyone else. I strived to be equal to, or even better than, anyone, including my peers.

This drive to prove myself made me incredibly competitive in school. I studied hard and aimed to get the top grades in every subject. Whenever there was a spelling bee or maths competition, I volunteered to represent my class. I slowly gained the respect of students and teachers as they realized I was smart and talented, regardless of my background. The bullying tapered off as kids came to see me for my merits, not just my differences.

Still, I was wary of letting my guard down. I remained vigilant against any hint of prejudice or mistreatment from classmates. That early bullying shaped me into someone who stood up for myself and did not let unfairness slide. It gave me resilience and a defiant streak of independence. I was not going to be anyone's victim.

As I got older, I started to see more clearly the complex web of history, culture, and politics that shaped Northern Ireland. The sectarian divisions, though real, were not inevitable. They were constructed by those in power to maintain control. The random hatred between neighbours obscured their common struggles. I learned that real change comes through communication, empathy, and recognizing our shared humanity beneath surface differences.

Though I stood up to bullying, I did not retaliate with more malice. Meeting aggression with aggression only breeds more violence. I focused my energy instead on excelling academically and pursuing interests like music, art, and computing where bias mattered less.

My experiences made me resolved not to judge individuals according to stereotypes. I would take each person as I found them, examine why people behave as they do, and spread compassion. While maintaining pride in my heritage, I would build an identity not limited by any group. Life's richness comes from blending the best of its flavours.

Key Takeaway

The difficulties and challenges you face in your life can either destroy you, or give you the motivation to push yourself further. The choice is yours.

3

My Father, My Mentor

After experiencing bullying, I received support and love from my mother and valuable lessons from my father. My father always told me, 'Life is like a show, and we must perform for the world.' My father was a very good driver, and he was always saying to me, 'You have to control the car; do not let the car control you.' This can be applied to life; he was teaching us the importance of being in control and not letting circumstances control us. These lessons about control and appearance stuck with me throughout my life, as I struggled with feeling different and vulnerable.

As a child, I was very active, curious, and mischievous. When I was four years old, I once chased a ball and ended up crashing into a glass door, shattering the glass and cutting my upper-right eyebrow. The skin was cut deeply and was hanging over my right eye. Luckily, dad was home, as mum could not drive back then. My parents took me to the hospital, moving as fast as they could. My dad said it was the scariest incident because I did not cry the whole time! Mum said she remembered how dad turned green with shock and fear. He ran through red lights, and later told me he drove so fast that exhaust fumes came out of the new Volvo. The engine had to be serviced later due to the rally-racing escapade. This was incredibly harrowing to my father, who was usually an extremely cautious driver. I remember sitting in the backseat, blood pouring down my face, as my dad drove like a maniac through the streets. My mom was freaking out, pressing a towel to my head, trying to stop the bleeding. But I just sat there calmly, not fully understanding the severity of my injury. The adrenaline must have kept me from feeling any pain. We got to the hospital, and I was quickly stitched up by a doctor. He said I was extremely lucky not to lose my eye. To this day, I still have the scar over my right eye, a reminder of my childhood misadventure. My parents were so relieved I was okay, but also angry at my recklessness. I had to be more careful!

Despite this mishap, my parents were always encouraging and loving, even if they didn't express it in a typical manner. I have not experienced any direct conflicts with my father, and I am uncertain if this is related to cultural or familial dynamics, or is perhaps the result of an Asian influence. Expressing my thoughts and engaging in sensitive conversations about feelings or challenging subjects has always been difficult for me. Even when I disagreed or felt hurt, I avoided confronting my father. Although I had lots of internal disagreements, we never had explicit clashes. I adapted by conforming to prevent conflict, enduring whatever came my way. This resilience may be an Asian trait, viewed differently for mental health reasons. While it may not be inherently good or bad, pleasing my father became a way for me to seek validation, love, and support through conformity.

My grandfather's strength and determination brought our family to this country, and we felt a sense of obligation to work hard and make him, and the family name, proud. However, this mentality placed a lot of pressure on me at a young age. I felt that any mistake I made would be a disappointment, so I tried to be perfect in everything I did. However, as any perfectionist knows, this is unsustainable in the long term. One never stops trying.

Patrick, as a teenager in Belfast, Ireland, pictured with his father in 1992

My father wanted me to become a doctor, dentist, or lawyer—a prestigious, high-paying professional that would gain respect. But my talents lay more with numbers and business. We had many heated arguments about my schooling and career path. I felt torn between wanting to please him and follow my own interests.

Through conversations with my father, I was eventually able to break the cycle of demanding expectations. This came down to realizing that the law was not the right career path for me and deciding to pursue work in finance and investment instead. This change led to healthier relationships in business, my personal life, and with myself. While my father's philosophy of total control was helpful at times, I also learned the value of vulnerability and flexibility in certain situations. As I grew and developed, I realized that the most important person to strive to be better than was myself, and that self-improvement was key. Sometimes, I needed to do things that might not be approved of in order to grow as an individual. Finding a balance between my own goals and the expectations of my family was a transformation that took time, but I learned how to navigate that balance and build a bridge between the two. My father became a significant mentor to me, offering guidance on education, business, and career success. However, we rarely discussed more personal topics like love or emotions; my father preferred to focus on the expectations and legacy that weighed on our family.

I found out that my father was diagnosed with cancer on the day of my brother's wedding in February 2016. The doctors had given him only a few months. I didn't share it with anyone on that day, as I did not want to share bad news on a joyous occasion. In the months that followed, my father was in the hospital and lost his ability to speak. In September 2016, I was torn about whether to go to London to list one of my companies on the London Stock Exchange, or fly back to be with him at Ulster hospital in Belfast. I asked him whether I should go, and he blinked, saying yes, I should go. My mother also urged me to go, interpreting it as a sign, and said my father would always support what I did at work. He always did.

Trusting this as a message from him, I reluctantly boarded the plane, promising to return the next day after the IPO (initial public offering). When I landed in London, Heathrow from Belfast, I immediately called my brother and asked how he was. He said the situation was not good, and I told him I wanted to speak to my father. He put my call on speakerphone, and I started to talk to him. As I was speaking to him, I could sense he was nearing the end, so I stayed the night with him at the hospital through the phone. I was talking to him all night, and I didn't need to say 'I love you'. Some things we did not need to say out loud, as they were all clear in our hearts. Actions speak louder than words. It is a very simple thing to say, but it was so hard. Almost half a lifetime spent unlearning some of his 'bad' habits. He passed away on 5 September 2016, surrounded by my mother, brother, sister, and about twenty family and relatives, crying frantically in the background. I just burst into tears and cried on the plane with my luggage, walking out slowly and trying to gather myself to get out of customs, immigration. I struggled to comprehend the finality of it all, feeling the crushing weight of guilt and doubt. Should I have gone or not gone?

Now, looking back, when I ask my mum that question, she says, 'He wanted you to go. He was so proud of your relentless dedication to your career and the family. That was more important than him.'

In the midst of my anguish, a sense of peace settled over me. I understood that my decision to pursue my dreams was a testament to the values my father had instilled in me.

With a heavy heart but a renewed sense of purpose, I made my way forward, knowing that he would always be proud of me. I found the strength to honour my father's legacy and make such a bold decision. That is a decision I would repeat every time. I have no regrets in life. If I did not go, that would not be considered a Tsangs or a Patrick Tsang move. It also reflected my upbringing and mindset. That is why I went on to continue the mission. If my dad could have spoken then, he would have said, 'Son, you have to go.'

Key Takeaway

Honour your family, be the best version of yourself, and make choices aligned with personal values, aspirations, and integrity.

4

Resilience

From a young age, I learned the importance of resilience from my father and grandfather, who instilled in me the belief that my family was strong and capable of overcoming any obstacle. This lesson has stayed with me throughout my life and has proven invaluable in both my personal and professional endeavours.

As I grew older, I refined and adapted this lesson to fit my own philosophy, but the core belief in resilience remained a fundamental guiding principle for me. In both business and life, the ability to persevere and bounce back from challenges and setbacks is crucial for achieving success.

I applied to many legal traineeships in the UK and Hong Kong. I always wanted to move to Hong Kong after graduation. It was my lifelong ambition; I wanted to go 'home' and challenge myself against the best and succeed, showing my success to my family so they could be proud of me. I attended many interviews in Hong Kong but actually did not get many offers. I always ended up getting rejected, mainly because of my Chinese language ability. I was interviewing at a time where fluency in Mandarin and Cantonese—and the glorification of Chinese culture and traditions—was of utmost importance. After 1997, when Hong Kong was handed over to China from the UK, there was a heightened focus on the centrality of the Chinese languages. I was brought up in the UK, I never learnt written Chinese formally, so my written language was weak. I eventually got an offer from a well-known city firm from London in Hong Kong, Slaughter and May, but they wanted me to come back the next year, even though they really liked me, as they had filled up their traineeships for that year. However, that would have meant going back to law school in Hong Kong for another year, which I did not want to do. I rejected the offer. From September 1998, I could not get a job in Hong Kong for six to seven months. Eventually, I went back to the UK for Christmas to spend time with my family. I was thinking that I would probably have to stay in the UK because I was not being able to get a job in Hong Kong. It was quite demoralizing. I knew I was smart, and I could not handle the idea of rejection. I was questioning myself. *Am I not good enough?* I went back to the UK and still ended up writing applications from there to Hong Kong, never losing hope. I was in Belfast at the time when I got an interview call from Hui and Lam in Hong Kong. I went back to Hong Kong for the interview and eventually got the job. I started on 1 April 1999, almost one year after graduation.

You have to be persistent and keep believing and keep trying. Not giving up is a trait that has served me well.

I did the Hui and Lam legal traineeship, which lasted for two years, from April 1999 to 2001. The law firm was a general practice—a medium-sized, local firm with no expats, all local Hong Kong Chinese, and no mainlanders.

In those two years, I did everything, from tenancies to intellectual property registrations, divorce, litigation, commercial, corporate work, and immigration applications. There were three other trainees. Working with the other trainees and speaking Cantonese every day was a lot of fun, and learning was so different for me. I had waited all my life to return to Hong Kong to find my identity and sense of belonging. However, ironically for me, everyone treated me differently because I was not seen as a local. This issue of not belonging there was part of my identity issue of being raised in the West and working in the East. It was a very surreal and frustrating part of life. I thought I waited all my life to 'go home' to Hong Kong and not be judged. Alas, yet again, I was not the same. I looked the same from an ethnic standpoint, but they thought I was more of a Westerner because of the way I spoke, acted, my body language, and even my habits and thinking. I was very unhappy and sad at the time because it felt lonely. I felt like I was an outsider and an outlier. No one knew about me or how I felt on the inside. Later on, this 'difference' turned out to be how I stood out from the crowd, and I managed to turn this into a superpower. Don't be held back by certain things in life, sometimes your weakness will turn into your strength. You just need to be creative and position yourself, or that trait, into something that is of value. Life is about creating value and getting yourself a seat at the table.

*Patrick on the day he was admitted to the
High Court of Hong Kong, 2001*

I always enjoyed working more than studying. In 1999, I was making about 1000 pounds, which is 10,000 Hong Kong dollars per month; it was very little. I did a lot of paperwork, clerical tasks, and also went to court and enjoyed it immensely. Some of the clients of the law firms had local Hong Kong celebrity clients, which was fun. Meeting famous people in person was new to me. I was in awe of them, but once you see them more, you realize that they are just another human being. Some are nice, and a lot are not. As I get older, I now value people because of their kindness and humility rather than their so-called fame. My principal tutor and master was William Lam, who is still a good friend of mine. I learned a lot from doing rather than from the people themselves. No one spends time teaching you stuff, you must learn on the job, which is very Hong Kong-style, and you have to learn quickly. No one wanted to train a random young kid. They just wanted things done. I embraced the challenge and thought the firm needed to be bigger for me to do more and perform more on a bigger stage, but I enjoyed my time there and made many friends and saw many new things, and time flew by quickly. I knew I was not in the place I wanted to be, and I decided to venture out even before the traineeship finished.

In 2001, I eventually managed to get into a new law firm in Hong Kong opened by a Chinese mainlander living there, Mr XJ Wang, a banking lawyer who used to work at ING Barings Bank. Together with two other mainland lawyers, they opened a law firm focusing on corporate finance and specializing in IPOs of mainland Chinese companies in Hong Kong. I thought the area of corporate finance and big deals was the way to go, and I immediately joined. I was not overthinking, just thinking that the area was very interesting and would give me an opportunity to be hands-on in finance. Unfortunately, they did not get enough business, and in 2001, there was another financial crisis. Business was not good. I was let go after three months. This was another devastating blow early in my career. I was rejected again, and the feeling was crushing. I was questioning myself. *Am I good enough? Or am I actually an imposter? Someone who just looks good on the surface, but people see through me?*

I shut down these inner fears and tried to focus on the positives. I then tried to search, and there were not enough opportunities based on my limited experience and 'chequered' background— as one interviewer said—referring to me not being from an international law firm. All the international law firms refused to hire me because of my lack of experience in international law firms, and many local firms were trying to cut costs.

Ultimately, I could not find a job for another nine months. I felt really low, embarrassed, ashamed, and useless. I had to pretend to my family and friends that I was still working to fulfil my role as the family's golden boy. The truth was I could not hold down a job. During those nine months, there were six or seven months I was out partying and drinking every day in Hong Kong's cool bar scene, Lan Kwai Fong. This is an example of how I turned a negative situation into a positive one. You might wonder, how can anything positive turn from partying and drinking? I was born, and generally am, an introvert. One issue that I had at that time was a general lack of confidence. I had not mastered the art of conversation, and that inhibited my success in life and business. My time in the bars of Lan Kwai Fong taught me that I could talk to anyone, whether they're male or female, sophisticated or unsophisticated, young or old—a little alcohol probably gave me a little Dutch courage. I refined my conversational skills and became a master. This is where I developed my networking skills, boosted my confidence, and put myself on the path to achieve the success I dreamed of (and got a few free drinks!).

I sat alone at many bars every night and with the help of some drinks, I managed to learn to approach and talk to anyone—men, women, old, young, and experienced—and I could strike up a conversation for a few minutes about any topic. I met owners, bartenders, and other patrons, often scoring free drinks. I learned one skill during that time, which was the most useful. There was no guidebook to this skill, just simple open-ended questions I asked, such as, 'Hi, how are you? How are you doing? Where are you from? What do you like to do?' The key is to always smile and try your best to make conversation. Making eye contact and listening and talking back. The key word is engagement, and that skill has now served me for the last twenty plus years in business.

Then, once, I had lunch or dinner with one of my other former colleagues named Kenneth, who was a senior partner at Hui and Lam, and was now working at another small law firm as a partner. He knew I was not employed and recommended that I join the law firm and explained to me that the pay was not substantial, but it would keep me busy and give me something to do. Kenneth, who is witty and intelligent, was very good at billing clients. A lesson that I learned from him that was extremely valuable was about value creation. When questioned by a client about charging $20,000 for a three-minute letter, he highlighted the value of years of education, legal experience, and a nuanced perspective on drafting. It was due to that experience that he could draft in such a short time. For Kenneth, it was about the value of all the experience he brought to the table, not merely billing for time spent on actually drafting the letter.

At that law firm, the main partner was Thomas. Kenneth introduced me to Thomas, and I worked as a solicitor for a year and a half in a small legal practice with no secretarial support. I was the only guy doing all the work, and I worked from eight in the morning until midnight or 1 a.m. every day. Even on the weekends, I worked nonstop. Thomas was detailed and brilliant, but also very stubborn, pedantic, and small-minded. He would micromanage every file, paper, and letter. I ended up doing everything, from typing to photocopying, to going into the core, to strategizing, to getting all the things done by phone calls and meetings. I ended up doing maybe five to ten people's work. That is what it was like during that year and a half of work and training.

It ended up boosting my work ethic and time management efficiency. Thomas was a crazy and imbalanced individual, and me being very stubborn as well, I ended up fuelling his demands. I did whatever I could to satisfy him, myself, and my ego, but that year and a half was probably like five to ten years of somebody else's. It was a bit like COVID-19, where one year seemed like ten years, and he made people cry in the office, shouting and cursing at them, so I developed a thick skin there. The lesson from this is that even though it was a torrid time that year and a half, I learned a lot from him and am forever grateful. I could take on adversity and use that to gain experience. The micromanagement was good for me from a training and learning perspective, but as a business owner, I have learned that if you get stuck in the details of each file or project, you will be sucked in and have no time to do other things. Priorities and time management are so important, that it can dictate whether you become successful or not.

During that time, I also realized that law was not for me; this was not what I wanted to do forever. Then, it was also another blessing in disguise that I knew this was not what I wanted to do. And that's why I felt that I had to do something different. I started to apply for other jobs in marketing and sales and finance, but no one would hire me because I was a lawyer without training, background, or experience in those areas. Some companies believed I was overqualified and would not consider me, even though I was willing to start from the bottom. My only other option left was to go for in-house legal counsel in companies. After a six-to-nine-month search, I ended up becoming one of the legal counsels in an e-commerce firm QI, an Asian conglomerate, and I was managing the European market. That was the end of the Thomas experience.

I have learned that quitting at the first sign of resistance or difficulty can prevent you from even reaching the door of opportunity, let alone being able to claim any rewards. There are always chances to quit and move on. It is easy to walk away from something that is difficult, and this happened a multitude of times throughout all the late nights and tough situations at the firm, but I was determined to follow through with everything that I took on. I always finish whatever I start, and I always try to leave any relationship in the best possible state. You never know when and how your paths may cross again.

When facing adversity, it is important to remember that you are just as capable and deserving as anyone else. So, when you are knocked down, you must learn to brush yourself off, stand up, and keep your chin high. Resilience is a valuable tool that, with regular use, can help you navigate and overcome any challenge that comes your way. In my experience as a human being and leader, resilience is a vital skill as it pushes you through challenges and uncertainties that arise through every part of life, whether professional or personal. Leadership resilience shows in how you adapt to change, deal with stress, resolve conflict, build a vision (often you have to re-evaluate that vision regularly), and build relationships with your team and partners.

Key Takeaway

Resilience is a vital quality for achieving success in both personal and professional endeavours.

5

Finding Mentors in the Business

While learning from notable successes is helpful, and gleaning their advice from their interviews, books, podcasts, and so on can certainly help you, it is a one-way relationship that will never be as helpful as a real-life mentor. Finding good mentors is vital. Remember, learning and education are two very different things.

You need someone who knows you, cares about you, can give you constructive criticism, help you through your problems step by step, and most importantly, inspire and help you grow. You need to learn from someone who has been where you are now. I was lucky—my best mentors lived with me and were around me all the time, sharing their wisdom both directly and indirectly every moment of every day.

If you are not so lucky to be born into a family of inspiration, you can find influential mentors in your workplace or elsewhere. The best mentors are people who are where you want to be. If you are looking for a mentor at work, try searching for people at a level (or several levels) above you in the company. Ask yourself why you admire these people—is it their speed, their knowledge, their competence, the way they can gain the attention of a room?—and then ask them personally how they built up these skills independently.

Then, use their advice where possible and applicable. Do not let the hard work discourage you; apply their advice to grow, and soon you will find yourself at their level (perhaps even surpassing them).

The best mentors are successful in their careers because their time is used well, so be sure to make yourself worth their time. Consider buying them lunch or a drink and exchange ideas. Their mentorship is valuable, so make sure it is clear to them that you understand and respect its value. At the very least, thank them genuinely for their time.

The Honourable Jeffrey Lam Kin-fung, GBM, GBS, JP, a Member of the Legislative Council and the Executive Council of the Hong Kong Special Administrative Region Government, and co-founder of the Hong Kong Ambassadors Club and BridgeME, is my mentor, good friend, and business partner. His wealth of experience and knowledge make him an invaluable mentor. Jeffrey is a mentor, an elder statesman, a successful businessman, and a well-established figure in the Hong Kong community. He is seventy-two—a couple of years older than my father. He is like a father figure to me. I learn from him, and I listen intently and carefully. His energy is beyond positive in how he shows up, as well as in his demeanour. He is full of positivity and optimism. I think I am a positive and optimistic person, but he is someone I look up to who makes me realize I can do more in those areas.

Jeffrey comes from a well-established family, with a grandfather who was a pioneering manufacturer in Hong Kong. They were one of the first to open a manufacturing plant in southern China and manufacture the yellow rubber duck and distributed it globally. His involvement in Hong Kong's Legislative Council and his business success is truly inspiring. He deeply understands the intricacies of Hong Kong's political and business landscape, and his insights and guidance have been instrumental in my professional development.

What sets Jeffrey apart is his genuine and authentic nature. He is a kind and approachable individual who has built a vast network of friends and trusted advisers. His time management skills are exemplary, and his emotional intelligence is outstanding. His schedule is packed with meetings, from breakfast to late-night dinners, yet he always finds time for everyone. He literally has five meals a day, one breakfast, two lunches, and two dinners, which is thirty-five meals a week. He always makes time to connect with people over a meal. Even on weekends, he remains active in his professional and personal pursuits, including golf.

I greatly admire Jeffrey's ability to balance his professional commitments with a fulfilling personal life. His dedication to his work and his unwavering commitment to excellence serve as a model for me. I strive to learn from his patience and observe how he conducts himself in meetings. His extensive network and ability to connect with people is remarkable, and I am continually learning from his example.

One thing that I respect and learn from him is his time management. He has an exceptional ability to manage his time effectively, juggling numerous commitments without compromising the quality of his work or the relationships he maintains. An example of Jeffrey's commitment to excellence is during a delegation trip to the UAE. He landed pretty late, around 10 p.m. After arriving at the hotel, he met with the rest of the group and got up for a 4 a.m. board meeting. After that, we drove from Dubai to Abu Dhabi at 7 a.m., an hour and a half car ride. We met with the Abu Dhabi Investment Office and during the meeting, Jeffrey and I had to sneak out and borrow a room in their office to conduct a media interview with CNN, and then returned to Dubai (another ninety-minute car ride) to meet with the *Financial Times* for another media interview. Thereafter, we met with the Hong Kong Economic and Trade Office for a short meeting and had sandwiches as lunch at the meeting, then we headed back to Abu Dhabi (another ninety minutes in the car!) for more meetings. After this, we hosted a dinner meeting with around forty people in ADGM in Abu Dhabi, including government officials and other prominent business people. After dinner at around 10 p.m., we drove back to Dubai, another one-and-a-half-hour car journey. None of us, including Jeffrey, had any time to rest, but he did not once complain or make a big deal out of it because his attitude was that he could do anything we could do. He did not even have naps during the car rides. That is the kind of attitude and way of looking at things I respect, and hope my teammates can learn from. We all try to look up to this and do it ourselves. I respect and admire him for that.

Patrick with the Honourable Jeffrey Lam Kin-fung, GBM, GBS, JP, and a Member of the Executive Council and Legislative Council of Hong Kong SAR Government, at the Legislative Council Complex (LegCo Complex), the headquarters of the Legislative Council of Hong Kong, 2023

An additional mentor of mine is Maurice Lee, who I met over twenty-five years ago. At the time, Maurice was a senior partner at the Hong Kong law firm Robertsons, whom I met in passing when I interviewed for a job there but did not end up getting. After leaving the interview, I held onto his business card, and we kept in touch. There was no formula or agenda. Over the years we developed a friendship, and our connection eventually blossomed into a mentor-mentee relationship, with Maurice providing guidance and support as I navigated this career and pursued my professional aspirations. Subsequently, he has been the chairman of the Arts Development Council of Hong Kong for many years. Maurice is heavily involved in Hong Kong arts and culture, and he has been a big cultural media figure in the region. Over the years I have been involved in a few aspects of the entertainment industry because of him. He was also instrumental in recommending me to become a committee member of the Arts Development Council. From over twenty-five years of not getting that one job, a negative turned into a positive. It was not planned, but when an opportunity arises, you have to see it, grab it, and like a plant, you have to keep nurturing it and you see the results over time. That is why I am such a believer in the long game. Beyond professional endeavours, our relationship extended to philanthropic efforts and community involvement. I assisted Maurice in sponsoring various initiatives and projects, reflecting Maurice's passion for supporting the arts and cultural scene in Hong Kong. Maurice has had an altruistic nature, characterized by his genuine desire to contribute to the betterment of Hong Kong's cultural landscape.

Maurice's selfless and altruistic nature is a defining feature of his character, as he is described as someone who prioritizes the well-being of others and the cultural enrichment of Hong Kong over monetary gain. His dedication and relentless pursuit of initiatives aimed at enhancing the arts and cultural scene in Hong Kong has inspired me to emulate these qualities.

In light of Maurice's profound influence, I strive to mirror his commitment to philanthropy and community enrichment, aspiring to contribute positively to Hong Kong's cultural landscape.

*Patrick with one of his mentors, Maurice Lee, partner of Maurice WM Lee
Solicitors, at the Tsangs Group Headquarters in Hong Kong, 2022*

That said, good mentors should not be in it purely for themselves.
A good mentor is someone you can learn from, who is willing
to teach. Every relationship is two ways. They should want to
see your successes accumulate just as much as you do, and they
should want to put in the time to help you get there. Find a
different person if they do not want to take you under their wing.

Beyond that, your mentor should be genuinely successful
and passionate about their work. Just because someone is above
you in the company hierarchy does not necessarily mean they are
more eager or skilled—it may only reflect time spent on the job
or professional networking.

You want someone who is always trying to improve and
better themselves and still striving for higher success. They should
also be able to teach what you want to learn in a way you can

understand—in other words, if you want to learn how to present ideas clearly, and they say doing so 'just comes naturally' to them, they may not be the best teacher of this skill (even if they are the most skilled on this subject).

One final note on finding a mentor—while teachers have the potential to be good mentors, I suggest looking at them as potential mentors with a grain of salt. Universities carry a veneer of gravitas, but I have found that all the education in the world may not compare to real-world experience.

Suppose you want to get real mentorship in business. In that case, you are better off learning from the successful small business owner who never went to college than you would be learning solely from a college business professor who never left academia to run an actual business. Most of the most intelligent and successful people I know never even went to college, or dropped out. As wise and helpful as my mentors and family were, they were not perfect.

Being under the guidance of an individual possessing greater experiential wisdom can significantly enrich your personal development odyssey. The prospect of securing a mentor is not contingent upon age; one can avail oneself of a mentor's guidance at any juncture in life. Finding a mentor is definitely a complicated and time-consuming exercise, but highly recommended. I do not think it is possible to find too many mentors in your life. You have to be lucky enough to find people that are better than you, faster than you, more knowledgeable than you, and willing to spend time with you to teach you and share with you their experiences. The reason why humans have done so well in the past millennium is the fact that they keep learning from the old generations, the previous cultures, and so forth. Humans have the ability to think about the future and plan things, which other animals cannot. Knowledge is then passed down to the next generation, and that is something that the other animals cannot do. The mentor's job is just the past knowledge that helps you save time, from not learning from your own mistakes. That's obviously something you have to do, but the mentors will help you speed up to learn things that will help you save a lot of time. And in fact, you will not be able to have the time and bandwidth to learn so much anyway. It is always good to learn from other people, especially people who are bigger, stronger, and better than you.

As wise and helpful as my mentors and family were, they were not perfect. Neither am I.

Key Takeaway

Finding a good mentor is essential for learning and growing, and the best mentors are those who are successful in their careers, passionate about their work, and willing to help you improve and achieve success.

6

Keep Playing the Game

Like many immigrant families, mine had high expectations for the next generation to do better than the previous generation and to achieve success. It is common for second-generation immigrants to feel pressure to live up to the dreams of their parents, who may have had to put their own aspirations on hold in order to provide for their children. In my case, my parents wanted me, from a young age, to become a lawyer or doctor, as they saw these careers as the most prestigious and financially stable options.

Growing up, I knew that I would eventually have to choose one of these paths. However, my parents, who had a traditional mindset, did not have much practical guidance to offer when it came time to make this decision. They simply expected me to work hard and become one of these professions to fulfil the family legacy.

In the end, I chose to become a lawyer, partly because it seemed more interesting to me, but also to please my parents and family and meet their expectations. I attended the prestigious and top law school in England, the College of Law in Guildford, which was a significant accomplishment in itself. However, getting into this program was not easy, as admissions were based on my performance on certain exams, such as the General Certificate of Secondary Education (GCSE) and A-Levels in the UK to get into university first. Only after obtaining a law degree with certain grades can one apply and get accepted in law school.

Despite my best efforts and discipline in studying, exercising, and meditating to keep my mind and body in top form, I did not perform as well as I had hoped at my A-Level exams when I was eighteen.

I received predicted grades of ABB for my A-Levels and got offers for reading law, including at King's College and University College of London, but ended up with BCC grades at A-Levels, which meant I had to attend Kingston University in England instead of my first choice, the London School of Economics. Kingston was not as prestigious as the other choices. I was devastated for the first time in my life. I could not believe I had not achieved what I expected. I even had my grades re-marked twice—because of the disbelief—but the results were the same.

To this day, I struggle to understand and accept why my grades were below my expectations and wonder what went wrong. I worked extremely hard (probably harder than anyone I know) and did everything that was expected of me, yet I still fell short of my goals. It can be difficult to reconcile the pressure to succeed with the reality of life's unpredictability and setbacks. The only reason I can think of was that year I took the exams, the examination board changed the syllabus, and the format was different to previous years. Otherwise, I cannot think of any other reason.

I was incredibly disciplined during those years with consistent studying, exercise, and meditation to keep my body and mind in peak condition, but I still failed. I was competitive and strong and did not take 'no' for an answer. I did everything my family wanted, I was in control and made sure everyone could see that, but still, I failed to achieve my goals. I did not know how to face anyone, especially my family. I felt like I let them down. I was a failure.

Sometimes, even the best-controlled cars perform poorly. My mentors did not prepare me for failure, nothing did. Failure was not an option (as per Eminem in his song, 'Lose Yourself') I had ever expected, and it was crushing. It hit me very hard, and I promised myself it would never happen again.

It was the first setback of my life. Looking back now, it's a matter of perspective. You are your own judge. No one really cares or bothers but your grades or university. All you can do is try your best and do what you can and accept what the situation is. Do what you can to progress and move forward. There is no regret. You cannot get all you want in life and never will, you just try your best and do what you can with all your heart and mind, and eventually the result will come. Consistent small steps over a long period will get you to where you want. People overestimate what one can do in a short period, say one year, and greatly underestimate the progress and results you can make over a longer period, say ten years. Therefore, it's always a long game. Don't let short-term setbacks affect you, which in turn could affect your long game plan.

When you feel weak and insecure about yourself, it is natural to want to hide your past mistakes or perceived failures. I know I felt that way when I went to Kingston University, despite having dreamed of attending the esteemed London School of Economics. But looking back, I realize that my experience at Kingston was just one chapter in a much bigger story. Encountering a setback early on is the best thing that could happen to me. It made me realize that life is not perfect, and I started to be more realistic and worked with what I had—what cards I was dealt with in life, just like in poker.

Throughout my life, I have achieved many things that I am proud of, despite not having the most prestigious degree. I have met royalty, heads of states, government leaders, and the most successful business leaders. I have interviewed some of the world's most influential people, climbed Mount Kenya at 5,000m, travelled to North Korea, Sudan, South Sudan, Tibet, Inner Mongolia, and Iran, grown a family owned restaurant and property business into a global family office, invested in the film industry, and invested in innovative companies that have made a real impact on the world, including a space tech project in Houston, Texas during COVID-19.

The truth is, grades do not define your worth, your potential for success, or your future. They may open some doors when it comes to job opportunities and your choice of university, but they are just one factor among many. I learned that lesson the hard way, but it ultimately made me stronger and more determined to succeed on my own terms. What doesn't kill you, makes you stronger.

I have, however, encountered many successful individuals who have never attended college, including my grandfather and father, but my family always had this belief that tertiary education makes one extra smart and successful. I've done it and been there, and I completely disagree with this thinking. I respect my grandfather and father, but I am also decisive enough to make my own informed decisions. Meanwhile, in recent years, we had a few summer interns from top-tier universities, such as Oxford, Boston, and the University of London, who were model students academically, at our family office. One of these interns was named Christopher (not his real name), who was a student at Oxford University. He was a smart kid, spoke multiple languages, and had been the head boy at a prestigious school in Hong Kong. However, Christopher made two major mistakes during his internship. The first was failing to show up for work on multiple occasions, and the second was not completing a task on time, which caused the team to miss a deadline. The previous night the intern went partying and called in sick during the deadline day and did not reply to emails or phones. No matter how late I went out in my younger days, whether drunk or otherwise, I would always honour what I said or promised, and in work, I never let anyone down. The intern not only let the colleagues down but also oneself. Nevertheless, they disappointed me with their lack of work ethic and attitude. Coming from a wealthy family or a good college does not make one entitled. College is not as strong a metric of value as one might think. Upbringing, core values, attitude, and hard work are things that are key in the game of life. In the end, I terminated Christopher's internship with immediate effect, not only because I was angry about these incidents, but also because I wanted to send a message to the other interns and employees that such behaviour would not be tolerated. Additionally, I believed that getting terminated would be the most valuable learning experience during the internship for Christopher. This was my gift to the intern. One that hopefully the intern can learn from. One does not get away with everything, and one should be responsible for one's actions. I wish the intern well. I hope the young generation can learn these simple yet important lessons.

From my acceptance into Kingston, I learned that I had to play the cards I was dealt. I could not 'fold' just because I did not find great cards in my hands. I had to find a way to win despite— or, even better, because of—the cards I currently held.

I could not change the grades I was given. I could not change not getting into the London School of Economics. I could not change who my parents were, the culture I was born into, or my heritage. I could not change that I was bullied, how I looked, and how I talked, but what I could do was work with what I had and find a way to win. And that's what I did.

I could choose how I reacted to those challenges and find a way to thrive despite them. And that is exactly what I did.

Although most situations are out of your control, you can still make decisions that serve you in your personal development and career. You cannot let one bad experience destroy your path.

Keeping an open mind for opportunities and experiences can benefit you. An example of this is from the midst of the pandemic, when I found myself back in Hong Kong, seized by a sudden urge to look into doing something different and revisit my educational pursuits. The world was pivoting rapidly to online platforms, and I was not immune to this digital shift. My days were spent researching various courses, seeking something that resonated with my aspirations. After sifting through an avalanche of information, the Owner/President Management (OPM) program at Harvard Business School caught my attention. I was previously accepted in 2008 at the age of thirty-two when I deferred due to the global financial crisis during the collapse of Lehman Brothers and Bear Stearns. Again, I was accepted in 2014, and I deferred because I had to list a company in London, and I could not afford to take the time away to study. Having deferred twice already, I told myself I could not apply for the third time and defer again. Despite the tight application timeline—I remember it was already August 2021, and the programme was set to begin in September 2021—I decided to take the plunge. Harvard Business School's reputation, its world-class facilities, and the vibrant community of entrepreneurs it housed were exhilarating. The programme, akin to an 'MBA on steroids', hosted an intimate cohort of 150 participants from all over the world, fostering deep connections. Over twenty years ago, I wanted to attend one of the world's most prestigious schools and finally I went. Never feel like it is too late to pursue something that will help you grow and keep yourself in the game. With my life and work experience, I know I can hold my own with any of my classmates at Harvard, which shows that the best teacher is out there at work and not in the classroom.

Now, looking back, I can honestly say that I would not change any of my past experiences. Even the difficult ones, like being bullied, have shaped me into the person I am today. I have to thank those experiences and the people who challenged me, because without them, I would not be who I am today. It is perfectly fine to be different, in fact, I now love being the outlier, makes me unique! Most important of all is to embrace and celebrate our unique qualities and experiences.

Patrick with his living group classmates at the Owner/President Management Program (OPM) at Harvard Business School, 2021

Key Takeaway

Never give up. Don't let the current bad situation affect you as you never know how your current adversities will end up pointing you in the right direction.

7

Follow Your Heart and Trust Yourself

Over the years, I have noticed a shift in my thinking patterns. Whereas I used to be more focused on short-term, concrete goals, I am now a longer term, more abstract thinker. This means that I am more inclined to consider the bigger picture and to think about the long-term implications of my actions. Another way of saying I am getting old!

This shift has allowed me to make more strategic decisions and to think more deeply about the things that matter most to me. It has also helped me to develop a greater sense of perspective and to see the world in a more nuanced way. Overall, this evolution in my thinking patterns has been a natural part of my growth and development, and I believe it will continue to serve me well in the future.

By year three in the legal industry, I realized that I could not continue any longer. I did not enjoy what I was doing, and I knew this was not for me in the long run. It was not a lightbulb moment, however; there was a slow build up. It was too restrictive for me. I had to follow too many rules, laws, and customs, and I did not have the freedom to make my own decisions. The lack of creativity and control came with the territory, and I knew that would never change. Leaving law was not a sudden revelation but a gradual realization over time. I was not motivated or challenged the way I would have liked. The financial rewards were not great (which never was my main motivator), the work needed to be more fulfilling, and the treatment in the firm was different from what I wanted. I needed a career that inspired me and gave me a sense of fulfilment. It took about a year and a half of persistent searching to land a job that suited me. This was a challenge as potential employers doubted my qualifications, perceived my past as chequered, and critiqued my written Chinese skills. With these limitations, I determined that transitioning to an in-house counsel role was my way out.

More importantly, I realized that I needed to make the most of my talents and find a career path where I could use my strengths to make a difference and be in control of my own destiny. I made natural progress from transaction-based law (mergers and acquisitions) to private equity investing. I was more interested in the vision, big-picture view, and relationship-building aspects of this work than the legal side of things.

After realizing this through my work, I knew I had to make a change. I changed schools and career paths, but it was not easy. Making a significant change like this is difficult for anyone. Coming from an Eastern family and being an immigrant made it even more challenging.

Reflecting on my university experience, I realize that I never had a true passion for law, but I chose to study it because it was what my family expected of me. Growing up, I was not encouraged to explore my own interests or passions. Instead, my focus was on doing what my family asked of me and following the path that my peers were on.

The difference between my peers in college and me was that they had a genuine desire to become skilled lawyers and pursue careers in the field. They had a passion for studying law and an ambition to improve their legal skills. They were asking themselves, 'How do I become the best lawyer or get into the best law firms?' and were motivated to do whatever it took to achieve their goals.

On the other hand, I simply did not care in the same way. While I did my best at whatever task was in front of me, I was more excited by the challenge itself rather than the subject matter. If it was not my passion, I would quickly become bored and move on to the next challenge.

In addition to this lack of motivation, I also found myself getting distracted and partying a lot after leaving home. In hindsight, I think this was a way for me to escape from the reality that I did not get to where I wanted to get to, and also, to compensate for how boring I found my new studies and new future career. I only went to the university library once, on the first day of school during the induction tour!

I did not study much during university, but I still managed to obtain an Upper Second Class Honours. This just showed me that working so hard didn't necessarily equate to the results one desired. I studied smarter and made use of time and made sure I had time to party and have a good time! That I excelled in!

My family had a hard time accepting my decision to change career paths after already going to law school and working in the field just because I did not enjoy it. It took them a long time to accept my choices. They were disappointed and felt like I was making a big mistake. Chinese people, or people in general, are creatures of habit. We would rather not change what is not broken. It was a difficult and emotional process, but eventually, they came around and supported my decision. My mother to this day still asks me why I changed and if I made a mistake doing so! On the contrary, I felt liberated and progressed much faster than I did on a path which was not right for me.

Making this change was not easy, but it was necessary for me to find happiness and fulfilment in my career and my life. I learned that it is important to follow your own passions and interests, even if they differ from what others expect of you. It is better to pursue a career that aligns with your strengths and interests, even if it takes time and effort to make the transition. And in life, you often cannot plan everything perfectly. You just have to take bold steps and see where it takes you and then work your way around.

It was a journey to find my true calling, but I finally found my place in life. It was not the path I had originally planned for myself, but it is a path that brings me joy and helps make the world a better place. It has also shown me that anything is possible if you believe in yourself and work hard.

I used my unique strengths to forge my own path, just like Bruce Lee encouraged. He was more than just a martial artist— he was a philosopher who believed in being the best version of himself. His teachings inspired me to break free from the expectations set for me by my family and society and create a life that was truly my own.

Key Takeaway

You have to do what is right for you, even if it disappoints those around you. It is your life. No one knows better than you. You will find success when you are doing something you enjoy, and the results will come in due course.

8

Life After Law

The two-year plus search (I had to apply for the traineeships even before I graduated from university!) for a job was both terrifying and exhilarating, much like my grandfather must have felt when he stepped on a ship to the UK. It was a frustrating and demoralizing experience for me yet, I soon learnt, a very valuable one.

Looking back, however, I can see that those two years of searching and struggling were actually incredibly beneficial for my personal growth. My former boss was a real taskmaster, and the pressure and stress of working under him forced me to rapidly improve my skills. I learned how to manage abundant case files, multitask, and work independently, all of which proved to be invaluable skills in my later career.

In the end, I ended up using my legal experience to move away from the law and into investment. In doing so, I avoided the trap that so many voluntarily walk into, what I term the 'golden handcuffs'. Golden handcuffs refer to what happens when someone becomes entrenched in a field that, while lucrative, is neither interesting nor impactful. The financial incentives are so high that people never move on or challenge themselves to try something new. While this may not seem like a bad thing, it was not the path I was destined for. I did not get the grades necessary for me to gain admittance into one of the top law firms, so in a sense, it was easier for me to leave. Many of my friends who ostensibly did better than me did pass that threshold, only to quickly find themselves locked into a restrictive, albeit lucrative, situation. They looked down on me when I was working in what they considered an inferior firm compared to them, but today I am the one hiring them and their expensive law firms! The process of avoiding the golden handcuffs was not easy, nor was it a direct linear path. I found myself between jobs, and for over six months I was unemployed. This was a particularly difficult time for me, not only because I was unemployed, but because I was ashamed to admit that fact to my family. I avoided telling them, going so far as to put on my business suit and bring along my briefcase when meeting with them for dinner. It was like something out of a movie. I have not shared with many people, but now I am open to judgement as I know that no one is perfect, and no one has a perfect life. I am proud of the fact I improved and grew over time.

The lesson was clear: in every situation, we have a choice to play the best hand possible and make the best of things. In Chinese, we have a saying, 'Once the boat reaches the bridge, it will automatically open.'

I went as in-house counsel at an Asian e-commerce company in 2003 and was fortunate enough to get it. This job proved to be a great stepping stone into the world of angel investing, venture capital, and private equity.

I was one of the legal officers, and I was overseeing the European market. The headquarters was in Kuala Lumpur, Malaysia, but the regional headquarters was in Hong Kong, where I was based. There were five legal officers, each managing a different region, and we all reported to the director of legal affairs. He was a busy man, often travelling, so I ended up spending most of my time in the finance director's office, working alongside him.

After working in the legal division for six months, I was offered the opportunity to move to join the finance director's new team, the investment side of the group. I became the second-in-command of the investment division under one of my mentors, Richard E. Zinkiewicz. This job was the foundation of my love and passion for the field, and I knew I had found my calling.

Richard was a great mentor and a true workhorse, and I enjoyed working with him and learning from him. He taught me many things and one of the most important lessons, the importance of asking two questions before entering into any argument or disagreement: Is the battle winnable? And is the battle worthy? If the answer to both questions is no, then there is no point in wasting time and energy on the argument.

Patrick with one of his mentors, Richard E. Zinkiewicz at LPM Restaurant in Hong Kong, 2022

Because of my challenging experience in the last job with the crazy boss, I found the work here relatively easy. I got the work done very quickly, and I soon grew bored and started looking for new challenges outside the work in the legal department. With the legal director often away, Richard relied on me to help him with legal issues and other tasks. I ended up working closely with him, and before long, I was running many aspects of the group for him.

My goal in life, including my time in law, was always to excel and find some measure of success. Part of it was to appease my parents, but I also wanted to prove to myself that I could succeed. In fact, pleasing my parents was really just a way of pleasing myself, and pleasing myself usually ended up pleasing them as well. It felt good to complete something and to do things well. It became a habit and a drug for me. Even after doing something very substantial, I would feel fulfilled but only for a short time, and I would have to go and find something else to chase. I left QI Group for two reasons: they did not honour what was promised and I wanted to venture on to focus on China. China was the story of the century, and I was not part of the train; I wanted to do more Chinese work. I was Chinese after all! I had been in charge of the new investment and fund division and had been promised a piece of the equity of the management company, but this never happened. I could not continue to work so hard for a company that did not honour their words and agreement. I wanted to move on to a company where I could grow and be more entrepreneurial, so I left QI and after looking at some opportunities, I became the general counsel of a Chinese venture capital firm. I had never done much in China, and I thought this was a good time to invest my time in the biggest market in the world, mainland China. A new challenge, a massive one, but had opportunity written all over it. I had never done business in mainland China, only in Hong Kong, a comfort zone. The Iceberg Theory came about because when I started travelling to China for work in 2006 and 2007, I was working for a VC firm doing a lot of Chinese work, and naturally I would learn more, starting from a relatively low level of experience. I went there; I had to drink a lot of high alcohol content Chinese wine, *Maotai*, get to know the people, establish relationships with government and business people and struggle with understanding regional accents, and learn the language in a business way. Now, I am fluent in Mandarin.

As you go more and more often, you become better friends with the people. We are all the same, after all, as human beings. Then sometimes you realize you do not fit in, as you may not understand all the jokes and the local trends, because people would have watched TV and listened to different songs from a young age, while I grew up in Belfast watching Hong Kong based TV dramas.

In the first five years of travelling and working in China, you immediately jump from level zero to level fifty and level sixty. You learn in the deep end very quickly in the first few years, but going from sixty to ninety is tricky because it's like an iceberg. In the first few years, you only see the iceberg at the top, above the water; you do not see the massive iceberg below the water. That's what I mean by the iceberg: the more I went to China after that, the more I realized I did not understand enough, the more I did not understand the nuances, the real meaning of what people think. This is all culture; this is all growing up there, knowing what people believe, feel, and want to do. That is what makes you a real expert. Sometimes, being a global citizen and having bi-, tri-, or multicultural experience will get you far, but you have to spend time there, which goes for anything. You must put effort and practice into things to get to the top. That is a true expert. You have to go in phases, but sometimes a lot of the initial learnings and ceilings are all on the surface and not deep, and ultimately, if you want to become a master expert, it has to be deep. This is the Iceberg Theory. To this day, I am still learning, and that's the only way to grow and progress.

After six months, I moved away from the role of in-house counsel and became a partner. I have been successful in this field and have been able to help a number of businesses grow and thrive. I am grateful for the experiences and opportunities I have had along the way, and I am always looking for new ways to challenge myself and continue learning.

My success and confidence were ever-growing, but we struggled to make money in 2008 when the global financial crisis hit everyone.

For example, we launched a chain of cinemas in northeast China to capitalize on the growth in the sector. Young people were making more money in China and needed to spend on entertainment, and the box office revenues were increasing circa 30–35 per cent yearly for more than ten years. We had a term sheet from Bear Stearns for $30 million, but did not get the funding because it went bust one week later! Luckily the business was a good cash flow business and continued to do well after 2008. We managed to sell the business and made a good profit.

In 2015, I returned to the family business, and we began to modernize and operate as a proper family office. I wanted to continue the family legacy and take care of the investments my grandfather and father made over their careers. As I mentioned, when my grandfather opened many Chinese restaurants in the UK, thirty to forty restaurants at one time, he began investing in real estate in Hong Kong and the UK. In the 90s, there were plenty of opportunities to invest in real estate in Shenzhen, China, and you did not have to pay a deposit to obtain a mortgage at the time. Throughout his career, he bought up commercial real estate in China, Hong Kong, and the UK and found great success.

After my father's death in 2016, I decided I would strengthen the vision and direction of the group for the next century. If I want to do something about climate change, then the best thing I can do is create a profitable company and use the money to do good things. We also dedicated more time and effort towards philanthropic pursuits. Our philosophy was better to turn a charity organization into a business, and then it becomes a money-making machine. And then the revenues of profits that you generate from that business will help the less fortunate people. It sounds like hard work, but it's hard work going back to people year after year and asking for more donations. So, sustainability works in two ways: in generating money and equipping people to be self-reliant.

The company has evolved over the years. When I first came into it, it was not very structured and mainly focused on real estate. Over seven to nine years, I have helped the company grow and evolve into a different direction, and we have matured significantly. We have made big and important changes. Now, we only invest in tech and innovation and do not make any new real estate investments—we just maintain and manage existing portfolios.

We focus investing in the following seven sectors: renewables, biotech and life sciences, artificial intelligence, robotics, mobility, software, gaming and entertainment tech.

Since I became the chairman, the company has evolved to do different things and to do things differently. Our key strengths are to see forthcoming changes and to act before the changes happen. That will help us capitalize on creating more value and mitigating any losses.

I am extremely proud. I helped the company start to do more things than just profit-making. Now, we are focused on win-win opportunities that benefit the world.

As the chairman of a family office, it is my responsibility to lead a team of like-minded professionals in making investments that create value and have a positive impact. Our focus is on early-stage investments, and we are committed to supporting companies that are developing innovative products and services. In this role, I work closely with the rest of the team to ensure that we are making informed and strategic decisions that align with our values and goals. I take pride in the work that we do, and I am dedicated to making a positive difference through our investment activities.

I am passionate about helping entrepreneurs succeed, and I believe that with hard work and determination, anyone can achieve their dreams. I am grateful for the support and guidance I have received from mentors and colleagues throughout my career, and I hope to pay it forward by helping others achieve their own goals.

Key Takeaway

Struggles and challenges lead to personal growth and can eventually help you find your passion. Each adversity or challenge allows you to learn more about yourself.

9

Reflecting on 'Integrity'

Credibility and trustworthiness are paramount. Integrity, the foundation of trustworthiness, is significant, surpassing any deal's magnitude. Money cannot purchase these virtues; restoration is a protracted one once your name and reputation are tarnished. It takes minutes or seconds to lose credibility instantly and can take a lifetime or more to recover. This symbiosis constitutes your brand, influencing others to engage with you based on the integrity and trustworthiness you embody. All relationships and business associations are forged not just through the transactions, but also because of the trust in individuals. This approach, a core value passed down from generations, is non-negotiable. Even prioritizing integrity over financial gains aligns with the enduring philosophy that losing money in a deal is preferable to compromising one's credibility, worthiness, and reputation—values ingrained in our family's legacy.

Here is an example of an investment that was innovative at the time but had difficulties because of COVID-19 and lack of integrity in the relationships in business that went south. I was approached in 2015 to invest in Aquavit London, a Scandinavian–Nordic concept. The first one was in New York City. 'Aqua' means water, 'vit' means life. The water of life.

The New York restaurant received three Michelin stars and did extremely well. They then franchised it to a Japanese group, and they opened it in Tokyo, which received one Michelin star. One of my friends at the time, Phillip Hamilton, who was Swedish, approached me and said, 'Look, I found this space. I have got this contract to get Aquavit to London; we can do something,' and I thought, okay, let's look at it. I looked at the space and I thought, everyone's doing Japanese or Italian or Chinese in London, so we wanted to try to do something different. This space was huge, over 10,000 square feet, over 1000 square metres, and three floors. I had the vision of scaling this to every major city in the world. We would have unique private rooms which central London lacked and excellent food and drink to cater for London's best.

The executive chef Emma Bengtsson was Michelin starred and well-known in New York. She came to train the executive chef, Henrik Ritzen, in London. Our London restaurant was awarded one Michelin star in nine months, which I think was the quickest in Michelin history. Warren Buffet came to eat and had so much food, which was a good sign! David Beckham and all the big stars from the UK came. Rihanna came two days in a row to dine in our private room. However, during COVID-19, we were closed for a significant period of time because having to pay for staff and the high rents were unavoidable costs, and we ended up losing a lot of money. I think we were shut for nine to ten months in one particular year, which was the first year that hurt us. We had to pay £600,000 in rent. In that year, we had to let go of some of the staff.

Though not deeply involved in day-to-day operations, I sensed the business needed to be on the right track. This shed light on one of the company's CEO, Phillip—it was evident that he engaged in financial misconduct. He was stealing money from the company, and we had to fire him. We had compensated him well with shares and salary. To add insult to the injury, instead of owning up and apologizing, he had the audacity to team up with outsiders to try to oust me. The situation exposed various issues within the business, such as the need for better management, robust systems, and the importance of not depending solely on one individual, necessitating the search for a suitable replacement. Phillip was not only the wrong person at the end of the day because of his weak ability but more importantly, he lacked integrity as a human being, let alone a trusted partner. When it comes to any time of business, always be prepared with an agreement to know what you want and where you stand.

Feel free to spend money and time on getting the best legal advice to protect yourself, otherwise, you will end up getting hurt when a dispute occurs. Another piece of advice to everyone is to assume that no one in business can be trusted. At the time, I ended up having to get more involved in the operations of the restaurant, which is what was not initially planned at the beginning. In hindsight, the project should not have been undertaken due to its flawed location and bad choice of management. However, recognizing this now is easier than at the project's inception. Even without Philip's misconduct, the venture might not have fared well. It's apparent now that the concept is not enough to attract the heavy hitting clients, as they prefer Japanese and Italian cuisine and suffer from an unfavourable location outside of Mayfair.

Ultimately, this was a test of integrity in how to handle relationships going forward, and it was vital for me to show up and stick to my own grounding. By regularly reminding yourself and others of this principle and actively working to incorporate it into our daily lives, we can make progress toward the same goals and uphold a shared integrity. It was also a frustrating and complex situation that brought up a lot of emotions. To manage situations like this, I use my Five-Minute Rule.

The Five-Minute Rule

The Five-Minute Rule serves as a guiding principle in managing our emotional responses effectively. This rule acknowledges the validity of our emotional reactions, especially when faced with challenges or setbacks. When negative emotions such as anger, disappointment, or resentment arise, it is natural to experience a strong urge to react impulsively. In these moments, it is okay to vent, express frustration, or employ coping mechanisms that help alleviate the immediate intensity of our emotions.

However, the key lies in the duration of these emotional responses. The 'five minutes' in the rule symbolizes the need to keep these reactions as brief as possible. It signifies the importance of allowing ourselves a controlled period to vent or express our emotions, acknowledging their existence, and releasing the immediate tension they create. This brief timeframe grants us the opportunity to process our initial reactions without allowing them to escalate beyond our control.

Once the brief venting period is over, it is imperative to transition swiftly. Prolonging negative emotions beyond this brief timeframe serves no positive purpose. In fact, allowing these emotions to persist can lead to detrimental effects on our mental and emotional well-being. Each moment spent dwelling on negative emotions only amplifies their adverse impact, infiltrating various facets of our lives, including our work, personal relationships, and overall sense of fulfilment.

I was disappointed and angry about the complicated situation with Aquavit and an untrustworthy partner. I acknowledged that someone within the business did not hold integrity. However, I then swiftly pivoted my perspective to think about what was left of the company and how to move forward. I decided it was better to refrain from doing business with people you cannot trust as partners.

Therefore, I urge you to embrace the Five-Minute Rule. By adhering to this rule, you will develop the ability to manage your emotional responses proactively, preserving your mental and emotional energy for endeavours that genuinely matter.

This approach to goal setting and self-improvement can be more effective than making resolutions that are often quickly forgotten or abandoned.

While finding my place in the world was a crucial step for me, I now realize that my journey does not end there. Rather, by starting from a place of integrity and consistently demonstrating qualities like honesty and resilience, we can not only achieve our own goals, but also make a meaningful impact on the world around us. It is important to remember that doing good for its own sake, rather than seeking personal gain, can be its own reward. By focusing on doing what is right, rather than trying to get something in return, you can build a strong foundation of principles and values that will serve you well in the long term.

Key Takeaway

Integrity is essential for personal growth and success, and it involves being credible, trustworthy, honest, and resilient as well as having a strong sense of self-identity. Also, implement the Five-Minute Rule during situations that frustrate you or make you emotional.

Part II

Empathy

10

Remember Your Roots

I went back 'home' to Hong Kong and began applying what I learned on my journey to the Tsangs Group. Creating a bridge between the East and West meant finding common ground, and one area of common ground was right under my nose: business. My goal was to elevate myself in the conversation of global leaders to be a trusted partner for companies and countries looking for a path forward, which involved me leading the Group into the twenty-first century. My approach was to diversify, adapt to the fast-changing digital world, and invest in new, disruptive industries in addition to our traditional portfolio.

I was particularly interested in investing in science and technology companies, as I believed they held the most potential for growth and innovation. However, I quickly learned that success in the world of investing required more than just following a set of rules. It required an eye for the unique and the ability to think outside the box.

I began to wonder where I could find unique investment opportunities. I did not have the insider information or connections that some other investors had, so I had to think about what unique strengths I brought to the table. It was not long before I realized that one of my greatest assets was my understanding of the Asian markets, specifically China, from growing up in a Chinese household to spending significant time in China. I knew what worked and what did not in the Chinese market, and I was confident that this knowledge could give me a competitive edge as an investor.

With this realization in mind, I began to focus my investment efforts on companies with a strong presence in China and other Asian markets. I spent time researching and analysing potential investments, looking for companies with innovative products or services that could succeed in these markets. I also made an effort to build relationships with industry experts and business leaders in the region, hoping to gain valuable insights and connections that could help me make informed investment decisions.

Ultimately, my understanding of the Asian markets proved to be a valuable asset in my role as an investor. By focusing on companies with a strong presence in these markets and leveraging my knowledge and connections, I was able to identify and invest in a number of successful businesses that might have otherwise gone overlooked. This included investments in film, cinemas, lottery companies, e-commerce platforms, and an online recruitment company.

'Think global, be local' is our Group's tagline which encourages individuals and businesses to dream big, have no limitations, and aim for success on a global scale, while also being very mindful of and adapting to local circumstances and needs. In today's interconnected world, it is important to think big and strive for excellence, but it is also crucial to recognize that the world is vast and diverse, and that there may be limitations or constraints in certain areas. As the Chinese saying goes, 'The mighty tiger is not as powerful as the local worm,' meaning that local knowledge and understanding can give someone a strategic advantage even against a more powerful opponent. This can be seen in the examples of Amazon being unable to surpass Alibaba in China and Uber ultimately selling its business to DiDi in China in the face of competition. To truly succeed in today's globalized world, it is important to balance a global mindset with a local approach.

At Tsangs Group, we strive to embody the motto of 'think global, be local' in everything we do. We have a diverse portfolio of businesses from both the East and the West, and we strive to be responsible global players. At the same time, we maintain a familial and close-knit team culture, with a strong emphasis on local, on-the-ground knowledge. When I was learning and observing how things were done in Hong Kong, I recognized the value of incorporating certain values and practices into our company without losing the benefits of our Western culture. As a result, we were able to blend Western management and creativity with local insights, resulting in a unique and effective approach. This uniqueness has often proven to be an advantage, as I have learned through my ongoing learning and growth.

My evolution didn't stop there. Eventually I began helping to bring Western companies to the Chinese market, before eventually growing into a truly global family office.

Key Takeaway

Balance a global mindset with a local approach to find cultural and diverse perspectives that will help you further in business.

11

Like Chickens Talking to Ducks

When I was at secondary school in the UK at thirteen, I started studying German as an elective at Campbell College, a prestigious boarding school in Northern Ireland. I have always had a knack for language learning and a good memory, and it showed in my grades. I was consistently one of the top students at school from a young age, but I was the top student in German class during the first term and exams. However, after the results were announced, my teacher, Mr Cooke, made a hurtful comment in front of the entire class. He said, 'How can you let a Chinaman come first? You all need to do a lot better.'

Everyone in the class chuckled, but I was humiliated and angry. I even managed to put on a brave face to avoid being seen as weak. It did not matter that I was the best student— Mr Cooke's words made me question my own worth and abilities. *Am I not supposed to be smarter and deserving of praise?* Deep down, I knew I was good, and better than the rest. I knew that I was just as capable and deserving of success as anyone else, regardless of my ethnicity or background. However, I also knew that discrimination and prejudice often stood in the way of people's achievements and opportunities, especially in those days. I was so upset by Mr Cooke's comment that I decided not to continue studying German the following year, and instead focused on other languages, such as French and Latin, which I also excelled in.

Despite Mr Cooke's 'Chinaman' comment, I did not grow up in China. I was born and raised in Northern Ireland in the UK (it's funny because people in England do not treat Northern Ireland as part of the UK and the people in the Republic of Ireland do not treat people in Northern Ireland as Irish, so I've been an 'outsider' anywhere I go). However, my parents were both from Hong Kong and instilled in me a strong connection to my cultural heritage.

From a young age, my father often told me stories about how wonderful Hong Kong was. He was very proud of Hong Kong, and he was very proud that he was from there. He was proud of his Chinese heritage, and he had a tremendous influence on me. When he was younger, his dream was to retire and take the family back to Hong Kong. However, funnily enough, when the day came to retire, he no longer wanted to return to Hong Kong to live! That shows that you have one idea, then you may think of other things you want, and then the target changes. He said Hong Kong had opportunity but also high intensity. It became too busy for him, and he ended up falling in love with the place he spent most of his adulthood, Belfast. 'In Hong Kong, if you can work hard, you can make it,' he said—and, of course, he loved the food and the people.

That all created a mirage of Hong Kong, which I was obsessed with. Honestly, I grew up thinking it was the centre of the universe. The more I could not have it, the more I craved it.

My family influenced me heavily to move back to Hong Kong, despite my Western training, education, and upbringing. It was our ancestral home and significant to my father and my grandfather. While working on my path, I always wanted to keep close to my family, and they still always and forever hold a deeply important place in my heart.

I may have gone against their wishes when I left the world of law behind, but that did not mean I did not respect and love my family and our history and heritage. Because of this, my growing skills in working with China, and the dreams of my family, I decided to return to Hong Kong to find my roots.

While my trip to Hong Kong was, in some ways, amazing, it also came with its own set of uncomfortably familiar challenges. In Hong Kong, like elsewhere, I was again not fully accepted. The Chinese idiom, 'chickens talk to ducks' in Hakka and Cantonese dialects refers to a situation where two people are unable to communicate effectively due to differences in language, culture, or understanding. I was seen as a 'banana', as someone who looked Asian but acted Western, namely, yellow on the outside and white on the inside. People could tell I was different the moment I walked into a room by the way I dressed, looked, walked, moved, and even by my facial expressions. This made me realize that it was not about my skin colour or ethnicity, but just growing up in Ireland made me different. No matter where I went, I was seen as different, and this would probably never change. I was either too much like a duck in a world of chickens or too much like a chicken in a world of ducks. No matter how hard you try, there are things you cannot change, and you just have to make the most of what you have.

Years later, when I returned to visit the secondary school, I bumped into Mr Cooke, who had the audacity to smile and greet me as if nothing had happened. I could not bring myself to be friendly with him and simply walked past him. It was a painful reminder of the racism and discrimination I had experienced, and I could not pretend that everything was okay. To this day, I still vividly remember the hurt and embarrassment I felt in his classroom. I cannot smile and talk to someone and pretend everything is fine. This person does not deserve my acquaintance or friendship. Over time, I have learnt to filter out such people and things—that add no value to your life and suck away your time and energy.

Despite the challenges I faced, I believe that they have made me stronger and more resilient. It also sparked a competitive drive in me to succeed and be better than anyone else, including myself, namely, to keep improving and be the best possible version of yourself.

But I realized, and more importantly, accepted, over time in my journey, that being in the middle of two worlds was not necessarily a bad thing. In fact, it was the best thing, I had adapted, evolved, and grown, by this point, to see my difference not as a hindrance but as a gift. In business, they always say to 'find your niche'. Well, I was born into a niche, a niche not many people were able to fill. My next step was learning to take advantage of that niche and strengthen and use my inherent gift.

I realized I had to find a bridge between the Land of Chickens and the Land of Ducks. More than finding a bridge, I had to build a bridge. I had to become the bridge. A bridge between the East and the West, between the past and the future, between the chickens and the ducks. A bridge from the Blue Sky of my youth to the new 'blue sky' of my present and future.

This helped me to bridge cultural divides and communicate effectively with people from diverse backgrounds. My differences became a source of pride and a valuable asset in my personal and professional life.

Although I initially felt self-conscious about my differences, I eventually learned to embrace them and see them as a strength rather than a weakness. At first, being different made my life more challenging, but as I grew my business, I realized that my unique qualities actually gave me an edge. My differences became a unique value proposition for my business and helped me stand out from the competition. I often say that a person's greatest strength is often also their greatest weakness, and this can be seen in the example of Muhammad Ali. His ability to take punches was unparalleled, but it also led to him taking numerous blows to the head, which caught up with him at a later stage in life and ultimately caused his Parkinson's disease. In the end, it is important to embrace our differences and use them to our advantage, even if they come with their own set of challenges.

My extensive knowledge of China and the East set me apart from those around me and made it easy for me to communicate across cultural borders. I was familiar with the customs, holidays, language, and etiquette of the East, which gave me a unique advantage in making deals with Chinese companies. My ability to leverage this knowledge made me a highly effective investor and allowed me to achieve results that others could not. In short, my expertise in Chinese culture and communication played a key role in my success as an investor.

Although I was familiar with Chinese language and culture, I was not a true 'local', as I had not grown up in China. This meant that there were certain aspects of the country that I may never fully understand or get completely right. However, I still made fewer cultural missteps than many others trying to do the same thing. While my mistakes may have been more noticeable to Chinese locals, they were often invisible to Westerners. Despite these challenges, I worked hard to improve my understanding of Chinese culture and minimize my missteps.

At the same time, my father said, 'You can't be attached to anything or any place. Go to where you think you will do well.' My father came to the UK to make money, after all, and send the kids to private school so his kids would not do what they had to do, and have the degrees and professional qualifications to avoid manual labour and low-level work.

I visited Hong Kong as a baby and a child on a few occasions, but I do not recall much from those trips. I was there again, notably, when I was four to attend the eightieth birthday of my great-grandfather in the ancestral village Lai Chi Wo in the New Territories, Hong Kong. I was playing and fell into a small drainage opening where the wastewater was flowing. I was crying afterwards, and my mother put me to sleep.

As I was sleeping, they had a banquet, and after the feast, there was a famous family photo of about thirty family members as a commemoration of my great-grandfather's eightieth birthday. My sister is in the photo, as she was the sensible one, not getting herself into trouble by falling into the drainage opening and then falling asleep! I missed out on the once-in-a-lifetime photo op by playing too hard! Sometimes, 'work hard, play hard' doesn't always work in your favour! Be warned.

I did not feel like a bridge until after I started to work in Hong Kong, I still felt like an outsider. It took me a few years to get used to the place, understand it, and eventually acclimatise. To be a bridge, I had to know both sides equally well. Globalization and the internet made it easier to do so because there was more need to have global people who understand different cultures and languages.

I certainly did not see the golden coloured Hong Kong of my father's stories. It was just a fantasy that Hong Kong was the crown jewel. My father had left Hong Kong when he was sixteen without much of an education and work experience. He spent most of the time in the village area, so his grasp and view of Hong Kong was all in his mind. For me, it was the Holy Grail that I had to get back to Hong Kong. Since I was young, I constantly got bullied; I just thought I needed to return to Hong Kong to escape it. I felt I needed to go where I came from and belonged, like in *The Lion King* when Simba returns to his homeland. Throughout my childhood up until graduating from law school, my sole objective was to leave the UK and get to Hong Kong. It didn't matter what I would be doing as I was sure I would succeed in whatever I did!

Sometimes, things do not turn out as we had hoped or planned. The reality of a situation may be different from our expectations and may even be worse than we had initially feared. In these cases, it is important to remember that we cannot control everything and that we must do our best to adapt and make the most of the situation. Rather than dwelling on what could have been or becoming discouraged by unforeseen challenges, we should focus on finding ways to move forward and make the most of what we have. By adopting this mindset, we can stay resilient and find ways to make the best of even the most difficult circumstances.

The best way, I thought, just might be to bring together the East and the West through the mutual language of business.

Furthermore, my goal was to do all this while using the inherent advantages of my culture and natural creative skill. I wanted to combine my grandfather's local restaurant familiarity with the multicultural tapestry of the future to find the kind of mixed success that was previously elusive. A world where chickens and ducks could put aside their differences to create a utopia that benefitted everybody.

Key Takeaway

Effective communication with others who have different experiences, perspectives, or language can be difficult. To overcome this, it is important to establish common ground and find ways to bridge any gaps in understanding.

12

The Differences Between East and West

As someone who has lived in both the East and the West, I have had the opportunity to observe and experience firsthand the many differences between these two cultural regions. While there are certainly unique characteristics that define each culture, it is important to remember that these are generalities and not necessarily true for every individual. That being said, there are a few notable differences that stand out to me.

One of the most notable differences between the East and the West is the collectivistic versus individualistic nature of the cultures. In the East, the focus is often on the collective group, with a strong emphasis on interdependence and community. In contrast, the West tends to value individualism, with a focus on self-interest, reliance, and personal achievement. This difference can be seen in many aspects of life, from parenting styles and education to business practices and social interactions.

Professional culture

Another significant difference is the way in which the East and the West approach relationships. In the East, relationships are often more formal and hierarchical, with a strong emphasis on respect for authority and tradition. There's even a term in Mandarin, *guanxi*, meaning relationships in business. They prioritize humility, stability, and the status quo. In the East, it is more common to accept and work on weaknesses and also takes a long time to develop partnerships and relationships. For example, Toyota has nurtured their partners in Saudi Arabia for over half a century. In contrast, the West tends to have a more relaxed and informal approach to relationships, with a focus on individual freedom, the present moment, and immediate gratification. While this 'in the now' mentality can sometimes lead to quick thinking and successful sales, it can also come at a cost when working with Eastern partners.

Finally, there are also differences in the way that the East and the West approach communication and conflict resolution. In the East, communication is often more indirect, with a focus on maintaining harmony and avoiding confrontation. In contrast, the West tends to be more direct and open in communication, with a focus on resolving conflicts openly and honestly.

Ultimately, both approaches have their pros and cons, and it is important to consider the unique strengths and challenges of each culture.

Language

Eastern languages, such as Chinese, Japanese, and Korean, are known for their complex writing systems and use of characters rather than an alphabet. These languages often have multiple forms of writing, such as traditional and simplified characters, which can create challenges for those conducting business in these regions. Additionally, Eastern languages often have formal and informal ways of speaking and writing, which can also create challenges for those not familiar with the cultural norms.

Western languages, such as English, Spanish, and French, tend to use an alphabet and have simpler writing systems.

These languages also have a more direct way of communicating, which can be beneficial for conducting business, as it allows for clear and concise communication. However, Western languages may not have the same level of formality and politeness as Eastern languages, which can create cultural misunderstandings in some business contexts. By understanding and navigating these differences and nuances, I was able to successfully bridge cultures and attain mutual success. On a deeper level, the actual structure of the respective languages speaks to the perspectives and norms each culture brings to the table. For example, take the sentence, 'Chloe and I flew to the moon on Friday, 7 November 2014'. In Western languages, the structure of the sentence is first subject matter, namely 'Chloe and I', and then verb and what we did, 'flew to the moon', and then the day, date, month, and year. In Asian languages, the sentence will read structurally as '2014 November 7 Friday Moon fly Chloe and I'. In Asian culture, my friends and I are the least important aspect of the sentence. The emphasis is on the bigger thing, and we describe the less big or important things in chronological order, namely, the year, the month, the date, day, the object, and then the subject. This means, that while the person will only mention themselves in the concluding verse in Eastern languages, in Western languages, statements are geared more towards individualism, always mentioning the person or object first. The perspective thus becomes 'me' vs 'we'. This affects business greatly, because if you adopt the western mindset in Asia, you will not succeed with Asian business partners. The trick of all this is to try to bridge your attempts to come closer together. Once you get to a spot where your interests are aligned, you are in a better position.

The psychological differences are subtle, but significant. It takes an intuitive understanding to grasp the implications of such innocuous things, especially when dealing with different cultures in business.

Etiquette

Western cultures tend to place a strong emphasis on standardization, training, and governance, and often rely on scientific and logical reasoning to make decisions. They also value constructive feedback and open communication. On the other hand, Eastern cultures may be more delicate in delivering messages and may prioritize the intention behind them over the content. For example, in the context of exchanging business cards, Easterners may aim to make it easy and convenient for the recipient by presenting the card in the direction so that the recipient can read the card when receiving it, rather than worrying about the card being upside down. Eastern cultures may also be more sensitive to criticism and may place a greater value on maintaining harmony and avoiding confrontation.

Several years ago, I attended a meeting in New York with Chinese partners to meet some American lawyers. One American lawyer, a typical fast-talking New Yorker, leaned back in his chair and threw his business cards across the table toward us on the opposite side without much consideration. While I am sure he did not mean any disrespect, this action was seen as disruptive and potentially offensive by the Chinese attendees. It is important to remember that cultural differences can lead to misunderstandings and unintentional offence, and it is always better to go out of your way to avoid such situations. In fact, the ancient Chinese military strategist Sun Tzu wrote in *The Art of War* that it is best to avoid confrontations and win battles without ever fighting. In this case, simply making an effort to present the business cards in a way that is acceptable and appreciated by the other party can help to avoid any negative thoughts or feelings.

While the lawyer in this case may not have faced any consequences for his mistake, it is important to note that such a simple error could have cost him a business opportunity. In Eastern cultures, it is common for people to be more reserved about voicing their feelings, which can make it difficult for

Westerners to understand and navigate these cultural differences. It is important to be mindful of these cultural nuances and to take care to avoid making mistakes that could have negative consequences for your business relationships. In many cases, a little effort and awareness can go a long way toward building strong and successful partnerships.

Team building

Team building can vary significantly between Eastern and Western cultures. In the West, new team members are often welcomed with open arms, while in the East, there may be a tendency to view them as potential competition. As a result, Western leaders focus on achieving immediate success and integrating the team for the sake of getting the job done rather than making friends. Over time though, in Western culture, new members will become part of the family—that is why they do a lot of corporate bonding to foster that sense of community. In contrast, Eastern leaders tend to prioritize building strong relationships from the start and maintaining harmony. The Eastern approach generally is more conservative and longer term when it comes to giving feedback; they do not want to voice their opinion that you are not good enough. They take longer to have that openness to give you criticism or comment on your work. It is only when people tend to become friends first or become closer that they are franker. This emphasis on relationship building is a key aspect of both cultures as it can lead to a more cohesive and collaborative work environment. However, the nature, goals, and sentiments of these relationships differ.

Eastern-specific focus on family and community

Eastern families tend to be more closely knit and have extensive networks, which can be leveraged in business more often than the networks of Western families. While both Eastern and Western cultures are evolving, Eastern families often have a 'kingdom' mindset, meaning they are more territorial and protective of their resources. However, Eastern cultures also value alliances and building relationships with other families, and often place a high value on upgrading their status and engaging with people who are higher up in the hierarchy. There is no Western equivalent, and so it is important to be aware of these cultural differences when doing business with Eastern families and to approach these relationships with sensitivity and respect.

There is a Chinese saying that wealth does not last beyond three generations, meaning that many families struggle to retain both wealth and businesses over time. To address this issue, modern Asian families have begun to follow their Western counterparts to create trusts and structures run by professionals (not family members) to manage their assets and ensure the financial security of future generations. These professional management teams are often better trained and more objective than third-generation family members who may not have the necessary skills or experience to run a business successfully. Western families are more open to creating systems and structures that are designed to ensure the stability and success of their businesses over the long term and hiring professional non-family members as senior management.

People from the East also have a storied history of immigration to the West, a drive to improve the lives of future generations. Take, for example, the fact that immigrants come together to support each other as they strive to adapt to new environments. The network aims for mutual advantage so that immigrants can send home more money and support their families. Of course, there are Little Indias, Little Tokyos, or Korea towns, but it is striking how there is a Chinatown almost anywhere you care to mention.

I would say Chinese and Asian people are natural networkers in a business sense, especially people from Hong Kong—similar to people of Indian origin, who go everywhere, make many different friends, and try whatever they can to make money. This is in the DNA, as is this entrepreneurial spirit, which is why we see so many Chinese and Indian immigrants going to every corner of this planet and laying a foundation for their families and future generations.

Problem solving

Eastern culture tends to approach problem-solving with more nuance and a holistic approach, while Western culture tends to be more practical and deal with challenges directly. However, this can sometimes lead to collateral damage that may harm relationships or offend people, potentially causing long-term harm. On the other hand, the Eastern approach aims to solve problems in a more comprehensive way, sometimes at the expense of taking much longer to address the issue. This can lead to a dilemma for leaders, who must decide whether to invest more time and energy in finding a solution that avoids hurting others' feelings or to prioritise efficiency and effectiveness in their company.

One way to think about this is by considering the difference between Western and Eastern approaches to healthcare. Western medicine, like taking Advil or Panadol for a headache, often aims to provide immediate relief but may have negative side effects if used consistently over time. On the other hand, Eastern medicine, like drinking herbal tea in Chinese medicine, focuses more on prevention and maintaining balance in the body. This difference in approaches can also be seen in the way that Eastern and Western cultures view the self and their place in the world. In Western culture, the individual is often emphasized, with a focus on 'me, me, me'. In Eastern culture, the individual is often minimized, with a focus on the topic at hand and a mindset that sees the self as a small part of the larger universe.

Simple values can have a significant impact on business relationships and outcomes. It is important to recognize that both Eastern and Western cultures have their own strengths and limitations, and it is up to each individual or organization to decide which values and approaches are most effective for their needs. There is not a one-size-fits-all solution when it comes to cultural differences in business, and it is important to be open-minded and adaptable in order to build successful and mutually beneficial relationships.

One example of how different cultures can learn from and adopt aspects of each other is the adoption of Japanese cuisine in Western culture. In the 1980s, when Japan was the second-largest economy in the world, they bought a number of golf courses and buildings in the US. This led to a surge of interest in Japan and a boom in sushi restaurants, as well as an increase in foreigners learning Japanese. Westerners even needed help using chopsticks. Nowadays, Japanese restaurants are widespread, and people are comfortable using chopsticks. This demonstrates how, over time, Western culture has adopted elements of Eastern culture and made them their own. The California roll is not a Japanese dish, but a Japanese dish invented in America.

However, in recent times, there have been a number of wars and political disagreements between various countries due to a lack of engagement and understanding between cultures. When there is more communication and understanding, there is often less conflict and disagreement. This highlights the importance of learning about and understanding other cultures in order to reduce the chance of conflict and increase empathy.

One of the pressing global challenges that we currently face is climate change and sustainability. To address this issue, it is necessary for everyone to come together and work toward a common goal. This problem is larger than any cultural differences we may have, and it is important that we put aside these differences and join forces in order to find a solution.

Despite the differences between Eastern and Western cultures, it is important to remember that we are all human beings and part of the same global community. As Bruce Lee once said, 'Under the Sky, under the heavens, there is but one family.' It is through learning about and understanding each other that we can bridge cultural divides and find common ground. While it is important to recognize and respect these differences, it is also important to remember that there is no one 'right' way to live. By understanding and embracing the cultural diversity that exists around us, we can learn and grow as individuals and as a global community.

Key Takeaway

The East and West may be different, but if you strive to find common ground, you can bridge cultural divides and find similarities in any situation. The alignment of interests can cross cultural boundaries and lead to successful partnerships.

13

Reflection: Bridging East and West

As I compiled a list of cultural differences between the East and West and observed them in my personal and professional experiences, I realized that neither culture was inherently superior to the other. Both had their own unique strengths and weaknesses, and their own set of cultural norms and values. In order to succeed as a global business and bridge the gap between these two cultures, I needed to be agile, adaptable, and flexible, much like water. My business needed to incorporate the best of both cultures in order to thrive in both markets.

During the early stages of my career, it was not immediately clear to me that I needed to bridge the East and West. At that time, I was more focused on establishing myself in my career and working hard to contribute to the success of the companies I worked for. However, my cultural background and language skills allowed me to work with Western clients at my first law firm, which was mainly Eastern-centric. This helped me to build strong relationships with these clients and gave me the opportunity to go the extra mile for them. Even today, many of these clients are in touch with me because of the rapport we established.

Later on, I worked for an e-commerce firm with offices around the world, mainly in Asia. This gave me the chance to meet people from a wide range of cultures, including the Middle East, Africa, and Southeast Asia. Working in a multicultural environment allowed me to expand my international perspective and become more open-minded and flexible when dealing with people from different backgrounds. However, I also learned that sometimes, despite good intentions, there can be a disconnect between what is said and what is actually done. This taught me the importance of being adaptable and being able to read between the lines in order to effectively communicate and work with others.

I also found myself acting as a translator, not just of language but also of culture. I was able to take direct feedback from Westerners and present it in a way that would not offend or distress Easterners, and vice versa. My intimate knowledge of both cultures made me an invaluable asset in this role, and I was able to use my cultural differences to my advantage in order to facilitate better communication and understanding between the two.

Finally, I found a job that felt more like a calling than just a career. I was able to use my unique cultural perspective and skills to help bridge the gap between the East and West, and to facilitate better communication and understanding between people of different cultures. I believe that by embracing our differences and being open to learning from others, we can create a more harmonious and successful global community. So, it is important to focus on the positive aspects of being the child of a famous person, and to use the opportunities that come with that privilege to make a positive impact in the world.

Key Takeaway

Ultimately, it is up to us to make the most of our situation and to work hard to achieve our goals, no matter how we may have come by our skills and opportunities.

14

A Global Company Born from a Personal Niche

One of the key factors in the company's growth was my ability to bring together the best of both Eastern and Western approaches. However, my personal strengths and values also played a significant role. I believe in upholding strong ethics and core values, and these principles carry over into every aspect of my life, including my work in the family office.

Throughout my career, I have always tried to do what is right and to treat others with respect, and this has not changed just because I have been in a position of leadership.

I have always strived to maintain a high level of integrity and to show respect to those around me, and I believe that this has contributed to the success of the company.

At Tsangs Group, we prioritize investments in industries and companies that not only generate profit, but also create positive impact and meaning. We believe that values, integrity, and character are crucial to success, and I am committed to upholding these principles in all of my actions. I am unwavering in my belief that respect and doing what is right are essential to achieving success, and I strive to embody these values in everything I do. Our commitment to value-driven investing and ethical conduct has played a key role in our company's success.

I want to make it clear that while I am an investor, I do not step into the role of an entrepreneur—but I am an entrepreneurial investor. Entrepreneurs are the ones who have the power to change the world through their innovative ideas.

As an investor, my role is to support and encourage these entrepreneurs as they pursue their dreams. However, I am selective in the projects and companies that I choose to invest in. I only want to be associated with ventures that align with my own values and goals, and that have the potential to make a positive impact on the world.

I believe that entrepreneurs have the ability to shape the future, and I want to support those whose vision for the future aligns with my own.

At Tsangs Group, we are committed to investing in innovative tech companies, including those working in fields such as renewables, biotech and life sciences, artificial intelligence, robotics, mobility, software, and gaming and entertainment tech.

Technology has always been a passion of mine, and I believe that it has the potential to solve some of humanity's biggest challenges, such as climate change. That is why we strive to stay at the forefront of innovation, and we work with companies that are pushing the boundaries of what is possible.

We are always on the lookout for the next big thing, and we pride ourselves on being ahead of the curve when it comes to groundbreaking concepts like space tech and blockchain. By staying attuned to the latest technological developments, we are able to position ourselves for success and stay ahead of the competition.

Networking is an essential aspect of attracting deal flow for our team. Building relationships with potential partners and investors can help to establish credibility and trust, which are crucial for attracting high-quality deal flow.

Having a strong network of people on the ground, particularly in the target market, can also be beneficial. These individuals can provide valuable insights and connections that can help to identify potential opportunities and bring them to the attention of the company.

Attending conferences and industry events can also be a useful way to network and showcase the company's capabilities and track record. A strong track record, particularly in the relevant industry, can also be a key factor in attracting deal flow. Potential clients and partners may be more likely to consider working with a company that has a proven track record of success and is viewed as a leader in its field.

We believe that disruptive innovation can come from anywhere and anyone, and we are committed to seeking out and supporting entrepreneurs, technologies, and changemakers that others may overlook. This may mean taking risks on new and emerging technologies or investing in companies founded by unconventional leaders.

Our goal is to be at the forefront of the trends that will shape the future, evolving from a small fishing farm village to restaurants, property and real estate, and technology. Being global is necessary to benefit the evolution of what we have done. We have gone around the world, from Hong Kong to the UK, back to Hong Kong, to Dubai, to the US, and to many other different places. As a global citizen, being this bridge does help us get access to deals, meet different people, get different ideas, understand different cultures, and get an idea of where the world is headed. Through this globalization, we have managed to create value, monetize, and then invest in different sectors. Going global is essential. We are constantly searching for and analysing the latest global innovations, and we only invest in companies and ideas that align with our values and that we believe will have a net positive impact on society. We are committed to staying true to our values while also pushing the boundaries of what is possible.

This takes a lot of research and a bit more time, but this data collection period is vital to making wise choices. Every investment is a risk, but it is possible to invest wisely, even in this unfamiliar ground of new technology.

However, while we diversify, real estate is still the bulk of the portfolio because it is generally how Asian families build their wealth. It was how my grandfather started, and it will always be a part of the company.

Keeping that tie to my family is a way of keeping the core values in place and to remind myself about what I am doing, as well as acknowledging and being grateful to the man who lifted our family out of poverty and instilled Eastern values in us. Eastern clients appreciate that and see it as a mark of credibility. I love knowing that we have such a solid core to the business. However, the world changes, and things change, therefore we have to, too.

Tsangs Group is an innovation-focused family office that bridges East and West. Our mission is to invest in global opportunities in technology which create a positive impact to make our world a better place.

At Tsangs Group, we practice what we preach. Our global presence, with offices in Hong Kong, London, Dubai, Abu Dhabi, Shenzhen, Seoul, and Singapore, allows us to bridge the East and West and connect with a diverse range of cultures and markets. We invest in technology in seven sectors as explained before, seeking out success in areas where others may not see value. This approach has allowed us to achieve more than my grandfather could have ever imagined, and it has also helped me grow as a person and learn more about the world.

Our team at Tsangs Group is composed of multidisciplinary professionals with a diverse range of expertise and cultural backgrounds. We understand that culture is not a monolith, and we recognize the importance of understanding and respecting the subtle differences between regions, peoples, and demographics in order to succeed in a globally connected world.

Rather than viewing cultural differences with disdain or worry, we approach them with excitement and curiosity, seeing them as opportunities to learn, grow, and make a positive impact on the world.

Our investment philosophy is not limited to a specific industry or discipline, but rather it is defined by our commitment to driving positive global impact. We use our multicultural expertise and opportunistic approach to deploy capital in scenarios where we can make a meaningful difference. Each of us is a bridge between the world we know and the world outside our doors. My advice to you is, do not be afraid to embrace your differences, as they may be what sets you apart and helps you achieve real success.

It is important to consider what your greatest strengths are and how you can leverage them in your work. This doesn't necessarily have to be limited to specific job duties, as even seemingly unrelated skills or experiences can be valuable in the right context.

For example, knowledge of Chinese culture and customs may not seem directly related to a career in investment, but it could be incredibly helpful in building relationships and understanding business practices in that part of the world.

It is also crucial to remember that you bring value to the table beyond just your skills and experiences. Your values and who you are as a person are just as important. As you navigate different cultures and environments, it is important to stay true to yourself and not lose sight of your own values in the process.

Key Takeaway

We believe that by bringing together a diverse range of perspectives and expertise, we can make a lasting positive impact on the world.

15

Stay True to Your Values

My understanding of Asian culture and customs allows me to effectively navigate business in the East as a Westerner. This unique perspective allows me to be a true global expert, adept in both the East and the West.

This is not without its challenges, of course. When I am in China, for example, I am perceived as being more 'British'. Likewise, while in the UK, I am viewed as being more 'Chinese'. While today this is only a matter of perception, this was not always the case. In fact, often this difference resulted in race-based bullying.

During my younger years, I was often bullied and treated differently for being different. I wanted to fit in and be like everyone else, and I took it personally.

However, as I grew and matured, I learned to embrace my differences and embrace who I am. Instead of trying to be the same as others or to prove myself to them, I realized that my unique experiences and perspective, especially my differences, were actually my strengths.

Now, when I am outside China, I am more Chinese and the Chinese expert, and when I am in China, I am more Western and the Western expert. People now see that my 'weaknesss' or 'difference' is now my superpower!

This realization has shaped my personal philosophy, which is a blend of Eastern and Western values and my own life experiences. I have learned that being different is my edge, and it is what sets me apart in my business.

Each of us has our own unique edge, and it is important to learn how to leverage it to our advantage. No matter what challenges we face, we should never give up and should always strive to turn negative situations into positive ones.

My Personal Philosophy:

- Our attitude when responding is the most important determining factor in life. If we have a positive attitude, we will always be successful. If you persevere, you will get through any hardship.
- Cultivate strategic patience, the ability to make careful, considered decisions with a long-term perspective.
- The idea of systemic limitations is self-prophesied and self-manifested. The only person setting the limits is yourself.
- Entrepreneurship is the same as any discipline, such as sports, music, and art; it is hard work and the passion that drives you, not the money. Money never drives or procures success. Money is just a product of good work.
- You can make the most out of everything just by playing the best hand that you are dealt with and it's all down to attitude.
- Time is of the essence; time is your most precious commodity. There are twenty-four hours in a day, use it wisely.
- We hold a lot of negative energy about our past. No matter what previous generations did, you did not do it, and we cannot judge ourselves by what other people do.

- Who is the most important is actually not your family, not your friends, not your company, not your business. It is yourself. You have to be healthy and happy to take care of any loved ones or businesses.

- You have to treat people with respect and conduct yourself with good manners. That is why the company is traditional and conservative in many ways, yet holds a progressive vision. You may have to unlearn many things that your parents and teachers taught you when you were young—without throwing out the baby along with the bathwater. However, the core values and teachings, which do not change over time, one should always hold close to one's heart until the day they die.

- I am a student of life. The journey never stops. The best way to learn is by listening.

- Life is like a game of poker. We are dealt a hand each and we do not need to compare ourselves to others, but to try our best playing the hand we are dealt with in the game of life. That is all we can do in life. Be the best we can, and we will have no regrets in life.

- You have a lot of ability on how to think at your own will, and that's where real innovation and creativity comes from. But the best of both worlds is to combine old core values with modern innovation, making a truly successful global citizen.

- Anything is possible.

While forming these values, I began realizing some slight contradictions in myself. I am a risk-taker, but I am also extremely careful. I am a control freak, but I am also very fluid and flexible at the same time, and I adapt to people to get the best possible result.

You may not be able to change people, especially over the short term, but the only person you can change is yourself.

I admit I am a workaholic; I am more than that, I am a lifeaholic! I want to live life to the fullest, stay curious, and want to keep learning. I value personal enrichment. I am a person who solves problems and values good results, but I do not place so much weight on exams or formal education and understand the power and beauty that can come with the freedom to make mistakes and learn from them.

I realized that these seemingly 'contradicting' values did not mean I am inconsistent. Instead, it meant I had finally applied Bruce Lee's lesson to its greatest extent. I had become like water. I would always be myself and hold firm to my core values, but I was adaptable under varying circumstances.

I knew a key that opened one door could not open every lock, just like how one strategy that worked for an Eastern client would not work necessarily with a Western client and vice versa. I knew when to use my strengths and when to work on my weaknesses. I knew when to mould myself to fit my needs, when to stand my ground, and when to burst through obstacles in my way.

Living a successful life, in business and anywhere, means adapting without losing yourself and your core. My grandfather adapted to the new world without losing his family ties. I lost my way for a while, trying to adapt to the world of law without regard for my passions and desires, but as I grew and learned, I found the right solution. Now, I have control over that aspect of life and can tell the difference between an 'adapt' moment and a 'stand your ground' moment. All this is thanks to my grounding and personality and strong self-esteem at the core of my being.

Key Takeaway

A key to success is to identify your core values, develop a personal philosophy, and stay true to your roots.

16

A Solid Core

As a global citizen, I understand the importance of being multifaceted and adaptable in order to navigate the diverse and ever-changing world around us. However, there are certain values and principles that will always remain at the core of who I am. These values have guided me throughout my life and have helped me to make decisions that are true to myself and my beliefs.

One of these key values is the importance of listening to my own gut and trusting my own experiences. I have learned that it is crucial to be true to myself and to my own values, even if it means saying no to others or standing firm in my beliefs. This has helped me to stay true to myself and to make decisions that are authentic and genuine, and it has ultimately led me to where I am today.

In addition to my personal values, I also strive to infuse my core values into my company and to ensure that we operate in a way that is aligned with our ethics and principles. Our company is committed to making a positive impact through our investments, and we have a philosophy of seeking out positive impact investments that reflect our values of innovation, sustainability, and togetherness.

We are very opportunistic and are willing to be flexible in order to pursue diverse investments that align with our values.

However, there are certain areas in which we will not compromise, no matter how lucrative the opportunity may seem. We will never invest in arms, recreational drugs, alcohol, or tobacco, and we will never support entrepreneurs who seek to bring negativity into the world. At the same time, we aim to disrupt the status quo and to challenge the status quo in a positive way. We believe in supporting the growth and success of our investments, and we always seek to ensure that any exits—whether through IPO or trade sale—are a win-win for all parties involved.

With these values in mind, we consider the following things when we are deciding whether or not to invest:

- **The development stage.** We invest in early-stage ventures. These are higher risk, and obviously, higher returns. We like them because we can influence the management and company more with our network, strategy, and experience.
- **The entrepreneur's ability (knowledge, execution, etc.) and integrity.** Is this person someone with values and principles? Is this person someone we can trust to execute their plan as written, not deviating from the agreement? Will they not misuse the capital for the shareholders and not just take the money for themselves?
- **The company's potential positive impact and positive influence.** We do not want to invest in projects that have negative energy. We want to invest in technology designed to make the world a better place.

Within the company's culture, we strive to uphold our values. As I mentioned, we at Tsangs Group like to practice what we preach. We are working on several of the U.N.'s seventeen Sustainable Development Goals (SDGs), which are a part of their global initiative to create a better world for everybody. These varied goals aim to decrease poverty, inequality, and hunger; protect animal life, and create a greener and more sustainable planet, among many others. In essence, they encompass the goals of humanity at large. I believe these goals are brilliant and are things everybody—but especially people in places of leadership like me—should take a good, hard look at. If your company is not working on any of these goals, either internally or externally, it should be.

Currently, the family office is working on SDG Goal Five: gender equality, Goal Ten: reduced inequality, and Goal Seventeen: creating partnerships to achieve the goal. These values are very important to me and my business. Equality and enrichment of community are values most people can agree on, despite their birthplace, experience, or beliefs.

To achieve these goals externally, we are investing in projects around the globe that have a positive impact and positive influence in these areas, such as plant-based foods, robotics, and AI. Technology, I believe, is our best bet when tackling humanity's biggest problems, such as wealth inequality. The advancements of technology and the advancements of the human race go hand in hand.

We are also tackling these areas on the home front—internally, not just via our clients. Goal Five, for example, is focused on gender and equality and is already successfully underway in our company—over 60 per cent of the company is female.

We do not have any pay gap between the genders, which we did not do by design but by paying what is good and fair to keep our people happy. We have four women in leadership positions, including our COO. Gender equality—all equality—is fundamental to overall success, and I am so proud of my company for already finding achievement in this area.

We will not stop here but will continue to promote these values as we move forward towards a brighter future.

However strongly I believe in my own and my company's values, I am not trying to convince you to take all these values on as your own. Everybody is different, and only you can decide what is important to you. You can listen to your mentors, and you can listen to me, but at the end of the day, you have to listen to your gut first and foremost. This is your life. You make your own choices. You have to approve of what you are doing more than anyone else, so you must determine—and adhere to—your values, principles, and philosophies.

As for leaders that are building a culture from scratch or those who have been in business for years, it is imperative that team members and leaders within your organization align with your company core values and principles. Each one of the team members plays a crucial role in upholding and embodying these ideals, and I urge you to make a conscious contribution towards this endeavour.

Actively integrating values into daily work, decision-making, and interactions, not only strengthens organizational culture but also fosters a sense of purpose and unity among the team. When we all operate from a shared set of values, it enables us to work cohesively towards common goals, ensures consistency in actions, and ultimately enhances our reputation in the eyes of our clients and partners. I encourage each of you to reflect on the principles that guide you and consider how you can personally champion them in your respective roles. Let us strive to be a living embodiment of what we stand for, both within our organization and in the broader community.

Upholding an ideal requires a certain level of commitment and accountability. For instance, if you strive for gender equality, you must put your money where your mouth is and take the steps needed to achieve gender equality in your business. Empty goals and words are meaningless and stick out to the customer. If you are not 'all in', your customers will not be either. You are the leader of the pack and the writer of your values.

Act like it. Make goals based on your values, then get down to business and work to achieve them. Your life, company, and the world will be better off for it.

Key Takeaway

Everyone has their own values, principles, and philosophies that they should determine and adhere to in order to be true to themselves and achieve their goals.

17

Financing the Climb

At our company, we believe in equality and strive to treat everyone fairly. However, we also recognize that not all ideas and entrepreneurs are equal. While we may not give as much consideration to an idea that is presented to us by an unenthusiastic entrepreneur who is only motivated by financial gain, we are more likely to invest in a well-planned idea that is presented by a passionate entrepreneur who has good timing.

We prioritize investing in entrepreneurs because we believe that they are some of the most influential and important people in the world. They are the ones who come up with innovative and potentially disruptive ideas that have the potential to change the world. That is why we are committed to supporting and financing these individuals and their ideas, in order to help them succeed and make a positive impact.

While I possess an entrepreneurial mindset and spirit, I do not consider myself to be an entrepreneur in the traditional sense. Instead, I see myself as an investor—specifically, an entrepreneurial investor, as well as a 'specialist generalist'. While that term may be an oxymoron, it accurately describes the value I bring to our partners. I am a generalist in the sense that I have an understanding of the holistic nature of running a business.

However, I specialise in supporting early-stage, high-growth organizations.

As I mentioned earlier, entrepreneurs are the driving force behind change and innovation in the world. They are the ones who identify problems and work to solve them, often through disruptive and innovative ideas. As an entrepreneurial investor, it is my role to support these individuals by investing in their ideas and businesses, helping to accelerate their growth and success.

Thanks to modern technology, it is now easier than ever for anyone to become an entrepreneur. With the availability of computers, the internet, smartphones, AI, and the constantly evolving new technologies, anyone can create their own website and access the knowledge and resources needed to start their own business. Many of these modern entrepreneurs are highly driven and passionate, in possession of the character and timing necessary to succeed in today's world. Of course, access to information has to be fully democratized. Today, the real value is in knowing how and where to apply that information.

One major barrier that many entrepreneurs face is a lack of funding. It can be expensive to turn an idea into a functional business, and not everyone has the financial resources to do so. That is where we come in. In line with our belief that everyone should have the opportunity to succeed, regardless of their current circumstances, we provide financial support to entrepreneurs who need it in order to bring their world-changing ideas to life. We do not believe that someone's financial starting point should hold them back from reaching their full potential, and we do everything we can to help those we believe in to overcome any obstacles and succeed in their journey.

We believe that great ideas should always be given the opportunity to succeed, regardless of the financial resources of the person presenting them. That's why we do not want people to be concerned about money when they present us with a great idea. We want them to be able to focus on their ideas and opinions, because that is what entrepreneurship is all about—solving problems and creating value.

If someone has a solution to a problem, it is likely that there will be demand for it, and they will be compensated for their efforts. By providing a capital injection to entrepreneurs, we aim to fast-track their journey towards solving problems and creating value. This creates a win-win situation, where the entrepreneur is able to achieve their goals and make a positive impact, while also providing a return on an investment for us. We believe that by supporting those who are creating value, we can contribute to a better and more prosperous world for everyone.

Key Takeaway

'Specialist generalist' investors like me support and invest in innovative ideas to accelerate their growth and success. The best partners believe that everyone should have the opportunity to succeed and make a positive impact, regardless of their financial starting point.

18

Ability and Integrity

When it comes to deciding who to invest in as an entrepreneurial investor, there are two main factors that I consider. The first is the individual's ability to problem-solve, make things happen, and adapt to change. While technical knowledge and expertise in a particular field is important, it is equally crucial for an entrepreneur to be able to overcome obstacles and find creative solutions to problems, whether it be climate change, food shortage, or other global issues. The ability to persevere and adapt is key to the success of any business. Even the best ideas can face roadblocks along the way, and it is the entrepreneur's ability to navigate those challenges and find a way forward that ultimately determines their success. That's why I look for individuals who have a strong track record of overcoming challenges and finding creative solutions to problems.

The ability to adapt and find solutions is critical for any CEO or entrepreneur to be successful. A rigid, inflexible approach is likely to lead to stagnation and ultimately, failure. Companies like Kodak, Nokia, and Blockbuster are examples of organizations that were unable to adapt to changing market conditions and ended up failing as a result.

Here is an example of a recent company we invested in, Rice Robotics, a service robotics and automation company in Hong

Kong, of which Softbank is a shareholder. Their only focus was the Japanese market. I was introduced to them through one of their shareholders and my good friend Steven Lam, who is the CEO and founder of GoGoX, Hong Kong's first unicorn. I was introduced to Rice Robotics' CEO Victor Lee, and after some quick discussions, I saw the potential in the company. We wasted no time and decided to bring their robotics solutions to the Middle East. By doing this, the CEO has had to adapt to a different culture. The Middle East and Japan are obviously very different, and also each market needs are very different. This shows you that you have to be open minded to accept a new market and open for business. Are they willing to do so? Are they willing to put the time and energy into this? It is a combination of both: Is there an opportunity and are you willing to adapt to put the business acumen into a different market? Will it be successful and are we willing to invest time and energy into it? So, it's much needed to be able to solve problems and to apply into a different scenario.

In order to thrive as an entrepreneur, you must be willing to be flexible and open to change. Your master plan must evolve over time, as you discover what works and what does not. It is important to be willing to try new things, learn from your mistakes, and adapt your approach as needed. This trial-and-error process is essential for growth and success, and those who refuse to participate in it risk becoming obsolete in a rapidly changing world.

In addition to ability, integrity is another critical characteristic that I look for when choosing an entrepreneur to invest in. Trustworthiness is essential for any business relationship, and I must be able to trust that the individual will follow through on their commitments, act in the best interests of the company, and be honest and transparent in their dealings.

We look for entrepreneurs who have a strong sense of self-awareness and authenticity, rather than those who adopt a 'fake it till you make it' mentality. It is not just about the idea or the entrepreneur's track record, but rather their ability to balance the interests of the company with their own and to find success through unexpected means.

Overall, the combination of ability and integrity is crucial for the success of any entrepreneur. Without both, it is unlikely that the individual will be able to build a successful and sustainable business.

When evaluating the integrity of an entrepreneur, I place a strong emphasis on their ethical behaviour and values. It is important to me that I can trust the individual to act in the best interests of the company and its shareholders, rather than just pursuing their own interests.

I also look for individuals who are willing to admit mistakes and take responsibility for their actions. It takes integrity to admit when something has gone wrong and to take steps to correct it. While it is natural to want to avoid bringing problems to the attention of others, it is important to have the courage and honesty to do so in order to address issues and find solutions.

I need to trust this person, to know their moral code, and to understand they will take up the responsibility needed to make things right in the interest of the company and the shareholders—and not (just) for themselves. When I meet high-integrity people who are ambitious, they will often be embarrassed or ashamed to bring up problems to me. They will try to avoid that conversation and do everything in their power to rectify or make it better before coming to me. That's not ideal but these are the kind of people you want to rely on. It's okay to make mistakes. We all mess up, but it's how we react in the environment that has presented itself with such challenges. It takes integrity to admit errors and faults. When I was young and made mistakes, I doubled my effort, energy, and passion for rectifying the situation before telling my boss or seniors. It's embarrassing to look stupid and weak, and it is always better to correct the mistakes of your own will, but you also need to realize when to ask for help. Be like water.

Overall, integrity is a critical characteristic for any entrepreneur to possess. It is essential for building trust and creating a strong foundation for long-term business success. In order to assess the integrity of an entrepreneur, it is important to spend time with them and get to know them on a personal level. This can involve in-person meetings, which allow for a more natural and intuitive understanding of the person's character, body language, and communication style. However, such as during the COVID-19 pandemic, it may be necessary to conduct meetings over Zoom or the phone, which can make it more challenging to get a full sense of the individual.

Of course, things like eye contact and directness vary with culture and cultural norms, so we always have to consider that, but integrity and ability both surpass cultural divides. People worldwide may have very different skin colours, cultures, and expectations, but we are all the same under the skin. I always say that if we cut our skin, we all bleed the same colour, no matter the culture, sexual orientation, or religion.

To gauge one's integrity, it is important to observe how they respond to challenges and mistakes. Are they willing to take responsibility and make an effort to rectify the situation, or do they try to avoid acknowledging their mistakes? Do they exhibit honesty and transparency, or do they try to hide the truth? These are all important indicators of an individual's integrity.

Ultimately, one's integrity is reflected in their soul, attitude, and sense of responsibility. By spending time with an entrepreneur and getting to know them on a personal level, it is possible to gain a deeper understanding of their character and assess their integrity.

Key Takeaway

Success in entrepreneurship is tied to the ability to adapt, problem-solve, persevere, and the willingness to act with integrity, emphasizing the importance of trust and ethical behaviour.

19

Humanity in Entrepreneurship

It is important to recognize that cultural norms and expectations can vary widely, and it is necessary to take these differences into account when assessing the integrity and ability of an entrepreneur. However, it is also important to recognize that, despite these differences, all people are fundamentally the same at their core. This idea has been reinforced through my own experiences and travels. I have learned that people from all walks of life and cultural backgrounds share many of the same basic characteristics and values. No matter where someone is from, or what their skin colour, culture, sexual orientation, or religion may be, we are all human and share the same basic needs and desires. I am certainly not in a position to place judgments.

For example, during a trip to South Sudan shortly after its independence, I was hosted by the president and had the opportunity to explore various business opportunities in the new country. My visit to Juba, South Sudan, was with a group of Hong Kong, Chinese, and British business people. We interacted with the president and other high-ranking officials. It was a surprise to observe the individuals at the airport, all armed with machine guns. We were all transported in SUVs surrounded by individuals carrying firearms, which was a noticeable cultural contrast. I am not fond of guns, a sentiment that also makes me uneasy when in the US. However, I recognize that possessing firearms is expected in a country undergoing significant changes. This is very different from my experience in Asia and Europe. Despite this cultural shock, other aspects of daily life in Juba seemed rather straightforward. I witnessed school children walking, dancing, and playing peacefully at school. The overall atmosphere appeared relatively calm, even though the landscape and environment were markedly distinct from those outside Africa. Ultimately, the people, like everyone else, shared similarities globally.

I have had the opportunity to visit and interact with people in countries with unique cultural norms, including the one and only 'Hermit Kingdom' of the Democratic People's Republic of Korea, or North Korea, when I was the president of the Rotary E-Club of Hong Kong and led a delegation with the Rotary Foundation to North Korea with about forty people. It was 2008 when I first embarked on a journey to the country, almost completely shrouded in mystery and intrigue. We took a flight from Beijing as there are not many direct flights to North Korea. The planes were old with propellers situated on the outside, like in an Indiana Jones movie! As soon as we landed in the capital of Pyongyang, we were received by the foreign ministry and escorted to the VIP lounge. To my surprise, we were allowed to bring our phones and laptops, despite hearing rumours that they would be confiscated at the airport. Obviously, all the phones and laptops had no signal. It was a very surreal experience as yours truly lost contact with the outside world during the entire trip.

As we waited in the VIP lounge, the deputy foreign minister greeted us with a warm welcome. The atmosphere was surreal, as if we had been transported back in time. The lounge was grand and reminded me of the grandeur of East Germany and the Soviet bloc. The leather seats were old, but well kept, adding to the retro feel.

We were then driven around in a grand entourage of old Mercedes S500 cars from the 1960s and 1970s. These cars looked and felt brand new, as if they had just rolled off the assembly line. As we drove through the roads, I could not help but feel like I was in a scene straight out of a James Bond movie. The drive was slow, peaceful, and quiet, allowing us to take in the beautifully trimmed trees and the monuments. There were no other cars around. People outside were working or walking, and they would peer curiously at the entourage of cars bypassing them.

We were taken to a massive mansion at the top in the middle of the city that was used to receive state leaders. Each of us had our own big suite, complete with all the amenities. One of the rooms had a piano, and we used it for entertainment during our downtime.

One of the highlights of the trip was a banquet dinner hosted by the foreign minister. We were served by beautiful servers, who could speak fluent English and Mandarin and, at the end, sang and danced, giving a world-class performance. They were excellent and multi-talented. It was a unique and memorable experience, one that I will never forget.

Despite these cultural differences, I have found that people in North Korea enjoy many of the same things that people in other parts of the world do, such as love, family, food, drink, art, and music. It is important to respect these cultural differences while also treating people with the same respect and dignity that we would expect for ourselves. It felt normal. I drank beer with the guys and talked about *The Lord of the Rings*. They were questioning me about Western culture and the outside world.

During subsequent visits to North Korea, I was able to participate in activities such as visiting shops, attending the Arirang Mass Games (the world's largest stadium and human performance), which is one of the most amazing things I have ever seen in my life, and talking with locals about Western culture and the outside world. These experiences solidified my belief that, despite our many differences, we are all human beings and deserve to be treated with respect and equality.

Fast-forward six years. In June 2014, I went to Iran with the Hong Kong General Chamber of Commerce, which is around 160 years old, the oldest chamber in the history of Hong Kong's organizations, for businesses to promote trade and finance. They organized the trip to Iran where they planned to take us to a few places in three cities, the only city I ended up going to was Tehran.

Tehran's largest hotel then was built by the Chinese, as the China relations with Iran were very good at the time. There were no foreign brands there. I did not see Apple or Samsung, all the cars were from the 1970s and 1980s. I was curious and enjoyed observing the people, the culture, and the place. The place was bustling with people and energy, but business wise it was very slow. People were very curious about foreigners. The mosques were very impressive. We met the chairman of Bank Melli, the biggest bank in Iran. I also met a lot of government officials, people in the business community, and a lot of young people, but because of all the sanctions at the time, it was very challenging to do business there. You may be wondering why I chose to accept the invitation to Iran. I had never visited it before, and I was intrigued by the culture that had sprung around an incredibly old ancient civilization.

I would have perhaps never gone on my own, but because the Hong Kong Chamber of Commerce had arranged the trip with the logistics and itinerary well planned, I thought that I could piggyback on it so that I could be a tourist and see what opportunities would be there. Everywhere we went, we received VIP treatment. I did not stay for the full week, I only went for three or four days, just to experience the culture and the people. Eventually, I left the remarkably intriguing place, where I ended up having dinner at the Chinese Embassy with the Ambassador. We were even drinking Maotai, a strong Chinese liquor with 60 per cent alcohol content, which was quite unexpected given the strict restrictions on alcohol in the country. It was a surreal and ironic experience. Years later, the Trump administration blacklisted eight countries, including Iran, automatically banning any EU traveller from obtaining the Electronic System for Travel Authorization (ESTA) waiver, which would allow me to get into the US.

Clearly—as testified by my passport—I had been to Iran, and years later, I was using my European passport to get the ESTA waiver into the US for my visa, which usually takes one minute online. I was travelling from London to Boston, and I had asked my assistant to get the visa, but she could not get it done. I was very frustrated and decided to do it myself.

As I was checking in at the airport at the British Airways desk in Heathrow Airport, somebody from Homeland Security came out to question me. They asked me why I had visited Iran and asked many questions, including did I make nuclear weapons or if I was a spy for the Communist Party! After the questioning, I found out that my waiver had been cancelled, I could no longer get the waiver. I ended up staying in London for a month to get my B1/B2 visa to the US. Although the trip to Iran was memorable, every time I went to the US thereafter, I would always get searched for two hours before I would enter. It was a very good experience but had a lot of consequences in terms of inconvenience.

One needs to balance the pros and cons in life and business. Not being able to go to the US is an issue, of course, but how many people can say they have been to Iran? Life is short, I take every opportunity I can to experience life to the max. It's a decision I made at the time, thinking it to be correct. If I have to bear the consequences of it, then so be it. The damage has been done and there is nothing I can do except to adapt to it. Hence the Five-Minute Rule! Thereafter, I got the global entry pass into the US. All I had to do was pay! I never got searched again! Where there is a will, there is a way.

My adventures might be an extreme example of what it takes to understand human nature, and the characteristics of diverse countries, but the lessons hold true. To conduct business in different parts of the world, you must understand the beliefs, challenges, and behaviours of various people, and be sensitive to, but not hindered by, the various political, social, and economic dynamics at play.

Regardless of where someone is from or what cultural customs they follow, they are simply people living their lives and striving for joy and success for themselves, their businesses, and their families. All people are equal and have the same inherent worth. It is important to recognize and respect these cultural differences, while also acknowledging our shared humanity.

Key Takeaway

Despite cultural disparities, respecting and listening to all cultures, while acknowledging our shared humanity, is crucial for fostering global business relations and mutual understanding.

20

Equality, Always

In my early career, I was fortunate to have a mentor named Richard E. Zinkiewicz. Richard held a philosophy of equality regardless of status and believed in a flat, outcome-focused organizational structure. He was a living example of this philosophy and did not expect everyone to do everything. He was a team player and would do a task himself if it was more beneficial for the group. One way that Richard demonstrated this philosophy was through what I like to call the 'we all pick up the poo' mentality. Pretend for a moment that while arriving at your office one morning, you notice that a dog has had an accident in the front lobby of your office. Would you simply ignore it and wait for someone else to clean it up? Of course not. You would pick up the poo, regardless of your status. I remember him always being willing to pick up the slack and do tasks that others might have considered beneath him. He never expected anyone else to do a task that he was capable of doing himself, and he set a powerful example for me as I began to develop my own leadership skills. Based in part on Richard's influence, I have carried this philosophy with me throughout my career in every level of position I have had and have always tried to lead by example, never shying away from the 'grunt work' when it needed to be done. While I do sometimes have to delegate tasks as a leader, I am never afraid to jump in and get my hands dirty when necessary. I believe that my authority as a leader comes not from my title or perceived status, but from my ability to be a team player and to treat everyone equally, regardless of their role or position. This is a motto that I constantly share with my team and promote that we are all equals, and that we support each other no matter the task.

My philosophy, 'anything is possible' is about empowering individuals to believe in themselves and their potential, and to work toward creating a better future for themselves and the world around them. It is about fostering positivity, resilience, and unity, and reminding us that no matter how different we may appear on the surface, we are all human beings with the same capacity for growth and success. By developing our skills, honing our integrity, and treating others with respect and kindness, we can create a world that is more inclusive, equitable, and compassionate for all.

One of the biggest challenges that many individuals face is systemic barriers, such as racism or gender and cultural discrimination. These barriers can be especially difficult to overcome, as they are often deeply ingrained in society and hard to change. For example, in the 1950s, it would have been nearly impossible for a member of a racial minority to become the president of the US due to the barriers of culture and racism. It took years of incremental progress and sacrifice to reach the point where this dream became a reality.

As I moved into positions of leadership, I faced choices about what type of leader I aspired to become. Should I rule through fear or benevolence? Did compassion make one vulnerable as a leader? I resolved that leadership devoid of care for people was not leadership at all.

My family's Confucian values that so valued hierarchy and order also taught care for the community. I believed strength did not require sacrificing human dignity. In fact, true leadership was measured by how we treated the vulnerable, not the powerful.

I aimed to lead through empowerment, not authoritarianism. Employees were given autonomy aligned with our shared mission. I saw my role as removing obstacles and enabling talent to thrive at every level. The goal was to expand the pie, not hoard rewards.

Leading with compassion required being vulnerable and admitting uncertainty at times. I learned to balance this with decisiveness when needed. People do not follow robots (we may invest in them however!) but flawed human beings trying their best. Build trust through honesty, not delusions of perfection.

While I had to make difficult personnel decisions for the health of the organization, I did so with care and consideration for those impacted. Every person in an organization plays a vital role. Treat exits with gratitude, not callousness.

Leadership offers a unique privilege to positively influence other's growth and fulfilment. Hold this responsibility as a sacred duty. Create a workplace culture that promotes mutual respect and a positive working environment. People remember how you make them feel. Lead from your heart. However, it is important to note that not everyone has the same opportunities to overcome these challenges. While some people may have the work ethic and drive to succeed despite these barriers, others may not have the same support or resources. This is something that we must be aware of and strive to address in our efforts to create a more equal and just society.

It is also worth noting that many young people today may lack the drive and determination that is necessary to overcome these challenges. They may be more shortsighted and focused on immediate rewards rather than long-term career aspirations. However, it is important to remember that learning and growing are essential to success, and we should all strive to keep learning and improving ourselves. We should also make an effort to communicate and maintain relationships with others, even if we do not always get what we want. This means being responsible and closing out any unfinished business or job offers, rather than 'ghosting' people or avoiding communication. By making an effort and taking responsibility, we can all work toward a better future for ourselves and those around us.

We have seen firsthand that not everyone has the work ethic necessary to succeed. We have had interns who excelled and others who struggled because they did not have the drive and determination to work hard. If you are young and looking to overcome challenges, it is important to develop a strong work ethic. While it is possible for anyone to succeed, it still takes effort to achieve your goals. Do not let a little hard work stand in the way of your dreams.

On the other hand, the idea that the upper class is protected and immune to setbacks and failures is a myth. Even those born into privilege, like many of my college peers from aristocratic and wealthy families, can experience setbacks and catastrophic failures. They may be more prone to these shortcomings, because they have not had to prove themselves as much as someone who comes from less privileged circumstances.

A good friend once told me that she believes treating life as war will make it war, and words manifest the mentality. She thought it was a negative perspective on life. I, however, do not agree with her. I do not think it is negative but rather realistic. Personally, I think life is a war. We have to fight for what we want, and we are not all born with the same advantages or opportunities. We have to fight every day, every second to achieve our dreams, but since anything is possible, the main opponent we have is actually ourselves.

Key Takeaway

We all have the potential to overcome challenges and achieve our goals with hard work, determination, and a strong work ethic, but systemic barriers and a lack of opportunities can make it difficult for some people to succeed. Leaders should strive to create an inclusive, equitable, and compassionate society that promotes growth and success for all individuals.

Part III

Self-Improvement

21

Be Mindful of the Past

Throughout history, times of instability have often led to shifts in the global power dynamic. However, these shifts have often only involved a rearrangement of the existing power structures, rather than a complete overhaul. For example, after World War II, the decline of European powers led to the rise of the US and the Soviet Union as dominant global powers.

While there was a change in the distribution of power, the underlying political, economic, and social structures remained unchanged.

Today, we find ourselves in another period of instability. Of course, the COVID-19 pandemic affected everything to an incalculable degree, but there is also political unrest in many countries. Examples include Brexit, US-China geopolitical tensions, 6 January 2021 attack on the US Capitol by Trump supporters, US tensions with Iran, and the Ukraine-Russia war. In recent years, we have seen a number of global crises and conflicts that have contributed to a sense of instability, such as border disputes between China and India and the US-China trade war. These events have had a significant impact on companies and economies around the world.

However, I believe that this period of instability may be different in an important way. The theme of decentralization is becoming increasingly prominent, and I believe this could lead to a new dynamic emerging from the current portfolio of crises. Rather than power simply shifting hands again from a superpower like the US to an emerging superpower like China, I believe we will see something different. I predict that the elite and influential individuals who seem to survive and thrive no matter the world's state will leap towards an even more decentralized and transnational existence. Corporations will become more and more influential and nations less and less so.

This is in contrast to the trend of globalization in recent years, which has brought people and perspectives together, but has also contributed to the rise of nationalism due to domestic political issues.

In the coming years, we can expect to see more innovation, progressive social values, and the emergence of new, non-state power bases. Companies are increasingly influential and are even surpassing nation-states in terms of GDP and influence.

For example, California recently overtook Germany in terms of GDP. The following 50–100 years will be dominated by AI, cyber security, digital economies, technology, and finance.

However, the opposite will hold for those not as fortunate. People do not accept change, usually. And it is these people who need help the most but lack the means to receive it. Rather than moving into a new, more accepting society, those left behind will turn inwards, deepening the rift that exists in nearly all modern cultures. We have already seen this trend play out in the US and the UK, with Trumpism and the Brexit movement—both of which seem to be backward-looking, regressive movements.

While it is often said that history repeats itself, it is more accurate to say that history rhymes. While the events of the past may not directly repeat themselves, certain elements can come back in a familiar way. In this case, the global power dynamic may not shift in the same way as it did after World War II, but all the same elements will still be present.

It is impossible to predict exactly how these elements will be rearranged and where the 'kings and queens' will fall, but we can be sure that the deck will be reshuffled in some way.

Key Takeaway

Instability in the world today may lead to a decentralization of power, with new, non-state power bases emerging and companies becoming more influential, rather than just a rearrangement of existing power structures, but not everyone will benefit from these shifts, and some may turn inward rather than embrace a more accepting and progressive society.

22

Embracing the Future and Plotting the Path Forward

It is my hope that the future will be bright and safe for all of us. However, we face numerous challenges as a species that threaten this possibility. In order to overcome these challenges and thrive in the future, I believe it is important that we start thinking of ourselves as one unified species, rather than as a collection of separate nations, states, and cultures. While it is natural for humans to have a sense of identity and belonging to certain groups, it is important that we also recognize the commonalities that bind us all together.

Now is the time for those who are committed to bringing about positive change to take an active role in shaping the global society of the twenty-first century and beyond. It is crucial that we work together and develop a coordinated plan that moves humanity forward, rather than allowing ourselves to be seduced by inaction and narrow thinking. We cannot afford to miss this opportunity to make a positive impact on the world and create a brighter future for all.

In the past, there were many barriers that hindered connection and communication between people, such as language differences, distance, and cultural differences. While trade routes like the Eurasian Silk Road did provide some level of connection between people, these connections were limited and often only accessible to a select few. Indeed, Marco Polo's trip to China was hugely influential because he'd gone farther East than most Europeans ever had, and this was unique enough to capture Europe's imagination. Even as the modern world began taking shape, it was rare for the average person to interact with anyone outside their immediate circle.

However, over time, the connections between the world's people have exponentially strengthened over time. While it used to be that only the odd merchant, soldier, or ambassador made trips across the globe, now many ordinary people travel for business and pleasure daily. It is also no longer a once-in-a-generation event for someone like my grandfather to move away from the village they were born in. It is common now for people to move permanently away from the country they were born in, in search for a brighter future.

In the past, such a move would have been a once-in-a-generation event, but it is now a more common occurrence. Overall, these improvements in communication and connection have made the world feel smaller and more connected than ever before.

Throughout history, technological advancements have played a significant role in increasing communication and connection between people. The invention of the printing press allowed for the rapid dissemination of information, and later technological developments—such as the telephone—made communication nearly instantaneous. These advancements also had a ripple effect on other areas of society, such as education, as more children were able to go to school instead of working.

Photography and television brought images from around the world into the homes of ordinary people, and the internet has further facilitated globalization in ways that would have been unimaginable to our ancestors.

It is easy to take these technological wonders for granted, as they have become a normal part of our daily lives. However, when we take a step back and consider the world we live in, it is impossible not to be amazed by the advances we have made. The technology we have today is truly miraculous, and it is up to us to make the most of this significant moment in human history.

We are fortunate to be living in a time when the power of the internet is at our fingertips. The availability of information and opportunities that the internet provides is truly revolutionary and has opened up a world of possibilities.

In addition to the internet, there are so many other exciting developments happening in this period of rapid human growth and development. Things that were once unimaginable are now within reach or even a part of our daily lives. For example, robots like Roombas and smart assistants like Alexa and Siri have become more common, and smartphones are now ubiquitous. The COVID-19 pandemic has also led to the increased use of video calls for business and communication, although it is clear that these cannot fully replace face-to-face interactions.

Overall, these developments show the adaptability and evolution of how we conduct business and live our lives, even in the face of unexpected challenges like the pandemic.

While the technological advancements that have already become a part of our daily lives are impressive, there are even bigger ideas on the horizon that have the potential to fundamentally change our world. These developments, such as colonizing space, fully transitioning to digital currency, and re-evaluating how our societies are governed, are pushing the limits of what is possible. We are fortunate to be alive at this moment of tremendous change, but it is up to us to have the courage to embrace it and actively participate in it.

While some of these ideas may seem ambitious or unrealistic, it is important to remember that even if we do not reach our ultimate goals, the collateral inventions and advancements that we make along the way can still have a significant impact. For example, the pursuit of colonizing Mars may not happen in our lifetimes, but the technologies and innovations developed in the process could help us address pressing issues like climate change and food shortages here on Earth. As Bruce Lee once said, 'A target is meant to be aimed at, not necessarily reached.'

Disruption occurs when existing technology is made obsolete by the introduction of something new and better. This has happened many times in the past, such as when we moved from horses to cars and from landlines to mobile phones, or when offline shopping was replaced by online shopping. It is important to embrace change and evolution, as it is a natural part of life and our environment.

That is why I am a fan of blockchain technology and decentralization. Rules and systems should not be treated as fixed, but rather should be open to change and improvement. This is our opportunity to think creatively, come up with innovative solutions, and take on global leadership roles. It is a moment where anything is possible, and I believe it is important to seize this opportunity and make the most of it.

Key Takeaway

Despite the challenges we face, there is an opportunity for positive change. Technology brings innovation, which is shaping a brighter future.

23

Be Like Water

I have always been a big fan of movies, including Asian movies, which is how I learnt Cantonese and about Chinese culture from a young age. Watching Hollywood movies positively influenced me, by making me more aware of general knowledge and pop culture, and also inspired me to dream as a young kid who grew up in a small city, strengthening the belief that I can accomplish anything if I put my mind to it.

I never had any formal Chinese language education. We spoke the Hakka dialect at home with family and extended relatives. How I learnt Cantonese is quite interesting. I learnt the language by watching Cantonese TVB soap operas at home on VHS rentals with Chow Yun Fat, Andy Lau, and Stephen Chow! That was our family entertainment and bonding with the family. Film has always held a certain allure for me, though my involvement with the industry has been marked by both success and disappointment. I first embarked on the movie industry as an investor, attracted by the industry network and potential returns. From 2007–2011, I provided financing for several Chinese TV drama series and Hong Kong films through a venture capital firm I worked at, and at some publicly listed companies where I was a director and shareholder. These investments proved to be very solid ones with decent returns in short periods, and we profited from a few wise investments like *Protégé*, a thriller that topped the Hong Kong box office in 2007.

After a few early success cases, I set my sights on Hollywood. In 2008, I invested in the Oliver Stone film *W*, a biopic about George W. Bush starring Josh Brolin. For this, I teamed up with Hong Kong entertainment mogul Albert Yeung of Emperor Entertainment Group, who is also one of the partners of Jackie Chan. I'd done a deal with him in the past and had made returns. I went to his office to tell him that we did very well with *Protégé*, and with that success I wanted to try to conquer Hollywood together. Mr Yeung at that point had never done a Hollywood deal. We were the ones that took him to Hollywood. The first movie that he invested in, in Hollywood, was actually with us, *W*. I syndicated and helped fund the $30 million budget, hoping to cash in on the election year timing when the contestants in the running assured that the results would mean the US either having its first female president or its first Black president. But the 2008 financial crisis crimped demand and as the film premiered during that time, it flopped at the box office despite critical acclaim. This meant that we, unfortunately, lost money. Mr Yeung and I haven't done another deal again, we've crossed paths and have said hello, but I think he still remembers that we lost money in the deal for *W*. We did well with *Protégé*, and it opened up opportunities with both Hollywood and Asian networks, so we were able to access a lot of deals. We had two scripts—*W* and *District Nine*, which was an excellent movie and turned out to be a box office hit. It is a shame that we did not invest in it because it was out of our budget at the time. We ended up investing in the Oliver Stone film, and still, we have no regrets. What is funny is that we got to know all the top players in the film industry. Sometimes, you win some, you lose some. Sometimes, it is down to luck and timing, but I have no regrets. The stars were not aligned, and we were not able to get to where we wanted to go. That's just how life is. You do not always get to where you want, but you learn from failures and your lack of success. In fact, you do not learn anything from success. It is only through failures and after many times of failing that you become successful.

This taught me a hard but valuable lesson. Timing is crucial to anything in life, including business. I did not regret investing in *W*, as we cannot control everything in life. After that, I decided not to continue in the movie business. It is a very tough business and I thought it was only worth pursuing in this sector specifically or any sector if you put 100 per cent of your time and effort into it. At the beginning, because of the success of *Protégé*, we thought we would do well with all the movies we choose to invest in. We actually had a particularly good script in Hong Kong called *Overheard*, which we ended up not investing in as we had our eyes set on going into Hollywood. Coincidentally, *Overheard* became the top movie in 2008 in Hong Kong.

We missed our chance at a double whammy. I do not think that I regretted not investing in *Overheard*, but it is what is this. I say I do not regret not investing in *Overheard* because even now, if I could go back in time, I would still would make the decision to invest in *W*. Oliver Stone is a top Oscar winning director, and Josh Brolin is one of the top actors in Hollywood and an Oscar winner. I think we were in a very unfortunate position of being in the wrong place, at the wrong time. Timing is the most important thing in investment and in business, and also in life. Sometimes, you cannot find the right timing. In such cases you just have to accept that sometimes things do not work out. You have to extract the lessons from these mishaps and move on. I do not have any qualms about doing *W*. It's just what it is. I actually moved on quite quickly from that, because I realized that there's not much we can do about the decisions we've already made.

What did I do next? I told myself that we were not movie guys. We decided that we would not invest directly in the movies again, unless we invested in a slate of movies.

Since my expertise and experience was in technology, I decided to focus 100 per cent on technology. People like Steven Spielberg or Tom Cruise or Jackie Chan are successful in this industry because all their energy and time is focused on their industry and nothing else. Unless one is willing to be a silent and passive investor, it is not worth the time and effort to be involved. The more movies one invests in, the more your risk is mitigated. If I am investing only in one individual movie or TV series at a time, the higher the risk. Investing in a slate of Tom Cruise movies is a much safer way than investing in one Tom Cruise movie. Not every Tom Cruise is 100 per cent risk proof. Hence, I decided to stay out for good. For the time being, anyway!

However, never say never, as they say. Around 2018, I caught up with a good friend and partner of mine, Oliver Mochizuki (another fellow global citizen, English guy who has Japanese and Irish parents), who produced various content, especially independent movies. We had dim sum for lunch, and he showed me the trailer of a project he was working on. I laughed so much and recognized its potential. That's how I ended up help bankroll an independent comedy documentary called *My Friend Tommy*, which is about a real life forty-year-old virgin finding his way across America. It took five years to produce, and doing it during COVID-19 was not easy. It was a rewarding creative endeavour, and multiple film festivals have picked up the film. The film is available for streaming on Apple TV (USA only), Amazon, iTunes, Google Play, YouTube Movies, and cable and satellite. It also won Best Film at Belgrade International Dok Fest (Documentary Film Festival) in 2023.

That led to my current foray into Saudi-made films with a well-known Chinese actor. I realized I could leverage the Saudi relationships to secure financing for movie projects. In 2023, I brought the actor to Saudi Arabia and orchestrated connections with key officials at the Ministry of Culture. With generous Saudi government funding, this paved the way for an unprecedented co-production agreement to shoot films in the Kingdom. We will develop content in Saudi Arabia. It is both a shrewd business move and a chance to strengthen cultural ties between East Asia and the Middle East.

We engaged with various high-level entities such as the Ministry of Culture, the Cultural Development Fund, the Film Commission, and the Ministry of Investment, after signing memorandums of understanding (MOUs). We were trying to use the film and actors as a way to attract more Chinese tourists to the Kingdom. The Saudi government was over the moon. It also marked the beginning of a relationship that aims to attract Arab tourists to Hong Kong and China. This is just the beginning and will hopefully be another bridge that connects the Far East to the Middle East and beyond. Another bold move by the Global Citizen connector.

My road to the cinema has been long and winding, with some potholes. But I have emerged wiser and ready for the next act as a producer. We have now set up Tsangs Entertainment Group—we are a boutique premier destination for financing entertainment projects and being the ultimate one-stop solution for all entertainment needs, with a particular emphasis on fostering diversity. We take pride in our dedicated focus on promoting and bringing Asian content to global audiences. Committed to catering to a wide range of tastes, we seamlessly integrate music, theatre, film, anime, animation, and live performances to create a harmonious and captivating entertainment experience. This is something that I have been trying to do for a long time since I was a young boy. I have watched TVB series dramas, movies from Asia, Asian stories from books and movies. And I wanted to share and tell these stories to my non-Asian friends. When I was a young child, I could never share these stories with my Western friends because they did not know who these people were and at the time, Westerners were not interested in Asian content. They often think the content is weird, and this is probably because of internalized racism; the West is seen as the default. Afterwards, I thought it was quite embarrassing to talk about Chinese stories because it was something different to the 'norm'.

Everything was always Superman or World War II, western influences and pop culture. In the present time there is Asian representation, and the timing is right. Asia is much more influential, and it works from a business angle—you can actually make money. We have seen popular Asian genres like K-pop have a huge influence on western markets. Groups like BTS have had enormous success globally and are perhaps even more popular than most Western artists.

I believe that we can add value by making good quality Asian content for the global audiences. That is why we have decided to bring Asian talent to Saudi Arabia, to make movies and to showcase this to the world. This aligns with my role to connect cultures, build bridges, both culturally and commercially. For now, the lights and camera beckon; no matter the role, I am eager to put 'action' back into my life in movies.

Key Takeaway

Being flexible and adaptable, like water, is an important quality to have in life. Water is able to adapt to its surroundings and take different forms, whether it is a liquid, a solid, or a gas. It can flow around obstacles and find its way to its destination. Similarly, being 'like water' means being open to change and able to adapt to different situations in life, including a failed investment or business concept.

24

Anything Is Possible—The Younger Generation

Through my *Anything is Possible* podcast I hope to spread the message of combining the time-tested solutions of the past with the modern improvements of the present and future. Podcasts themselves are a perfect example of this, as they take an old concept (radio talk shows) and bring them into the modern era through their availability (on demand) and accessibility on various platforms.

I saw how Hong Kong had been affected negatively by social protests and COVID-19 and decided to interview a few influential friends to inspire the young people in Hong Kong. After we finished a few episodes with no external team or experience, I thought it should not be restricted to Hong Kong but should be shared with the youth of the world and beyond. I also became more efficient online with staff and partners, resulting in a need to travel less (saving time and emissions and being better for the planet). The show is about sharing positivity, overcoming challenges, and creating One World together. We ended up interviewing almost 100 guests, ranging from global leaders, celebrities, influencers, moguls, entrepreneurs, and more about their journey to success. You may recognize some guests, considering the guest list includes names like: Anthony Scaramucci, former White House communications director, founder and managing partner of Skybridge Capital, and founder and chairman of SALT; Melissa Rivers, *New York Times* bestselling author, award-winning writer, host, and producer; Richard Turner, the most skilled card mechanic of our time; Caroline Rush, CEO of the British Fashion Council; Tim Draper, Silicon Valley venture capitalist, the founding partner of Draper Associates; Dr Malvika Iyer, an international motivational speaker and disability rights activist; Komal Ahmad, founder of Copia; John Barnes, former Liverpool and England footballer; Jim Rogers, an American investor and financial commentator; Brock Pierce, philanthropist, entrepreneur, impact investor, and chairman of Bitcoin Foundation; and neo-pop surrealist artist Philip Colbert.

Patrick with Anything is Possible *podcast guest Melissa Rivers, New York Times bestselling author, Award-Winning writer, host, and producer in Los Angeles, 2022*

One of my goals with this podcast is to empower and educate young people, following in the footsteps of my great-grandfather and the generations that came after him, who all believed that education is the key to success. If I can use my platform to inspire even one person to develop the skills needed to achieve their dreams, it could have a positive ripple effect.

I believe that by embracing the lessons and values of the past while embracing the possibilities of the present and future, we can create a brighter and more equitable future for all.

The young generation is our future, and it is essential that we support and empower them to become leaders and problem-solvers. With the right guidance and resources, they have the potential to address pressing issues such as sustainability, climate change, and food shortages. It would be a mistake to ignore the potential of young people, who will one day create technology and art that will dictate the developments of the future.

As mentors to the younger generation, it is our responsibility to encourage them to take control of their own lives, embrace a strong work ethic, and strive to create a better future for all. We must not underestimate the power and potential of the young people around us, as they have the ability to drive positive change and make anything possible.

As a mentor, it is important for me to guide young people toward a more community-focused mindset and encourage them to think beyond their own interests. We must draw inspiration from the dreams of our ancestors and pass them on to the younger generations, while also embracing the best of both the East and the West, the past and the future.

To create a better future, it is necessary to learn from the mistakes of the past, both on a cultural and personal level. This includes acknowledging and addressing any biases or prejudices that we may have inherited from our family or community, and learning to forgive ourselves for our own mistakes in order to move forward with strength and resilience. It is through acknowledging and addressing these challenges that we can grow and become the best versions of ourselves.

I want to tell you about a question I asked one of my podcast guests and good friend, Richard Turner, the most skilled card mechanic and magician of our time. Richard lost his sight at the age of nine from Charles Bonnet Syndrome—a medical condition in which one experiences visual hallucinations caused by the brain's adjustment to significant vision loss. Even though he is blind, he can do with cards what no one on the planet can, and he achieved this through sheer hard work. He was obsessed and would have cards with him twenty-four hours a day and seven days a week. We joked that if it was up to him, he would make love to his wife with his cards in his hands! I asked him if he was not blind, would he still be as good as he is and the best in the industry? He answered that he would never have been as good if he was normal. The blindness caused him to go to extreme measures to be the best. He does not like it when people look down on him and tell him what he can and cannot do. He does not see images in the back of the brain like people who can see do when they dream or imagine things.

> I see them in an external space. I see them in front of me just as clearly as you know what is before you. And these reds, blues, yellows, and greens are just as vivid. If my eyes are open or closed, if it's a pitch-black night locked in a vault, probably the simplest way to explain how I see is I can write in the air, say I want to remember a phone number. I can write the phone number down in the air. I will see it floating in the air just like you would see it on a computer screen or whiteboard. My mind takes a picture of it. Because as I said, I was called an eidetic memory. I always remember it. I want my work to stand on its own against any other person. Two-legged, one-legged, whatever, I want my work to stand on its own. I never was a fan of handicaps, but it makes it suitable. That was how it was for most of my life until my wife told me to get over myself and start opening up and sharing my life experiences

and challenges with others because you can recruit others to deal with the situation they are going through.

Richard is the epitome of what 'anything is possible' means. He has not let his challenge of being blind diminish his purpose or power. He can outperform anyone off the street.

It is important to strike a balance between the past and the future in order to achieve our goals, whatever they may be. By staying grounded in our past and tapping into the wisdom of our ancestors, we can make informed and strategic decisions for the present and future. At the same time, we must also be open to new advancements and opportunities, as they can help us shape the future in a positive way.

Through my podcast, I aim to share this message with the younger generation and encourage them to embrace the best of both the past and the future. This applies not only in business, but also in many other areas of life. By learning from the patterns and themes of the past and being proactive in anticipating the new developments of the future, we can make informed decisions and navigate our way through an exciting, yet uncertain world.

Also, we must learn from personal mistakes—and I do not only mean this in one's business or career. I probably should have let go of the racism and bullying I faced earlier than I did. It was not my fault, it was someone else's fault, yet I let that pain eat away at me for years.

It is also essential to always keep empathy in mind, as it helps us consider the needs and perspectives of others, whether they are our colleagues, clients, or even competitors. By being empathetic toward others, we can better understand and navigate the complexities of the world around us.

We all must start from somewhere, and for most of us this means starting from scratch. People often mistake a beginner's mind as a mind that is limited or undeveloped. However, a beginner's mind does not mean discarding knowledge or regressing. On the contrary, it allows us to build understanding and circle topics at ever-higher levels. The goal is dynamism, not ignorance. Cultivating a beginner's mind requires humility. Park your ego at the door and you gain access to spaces otherwise barred. Develop expertise while retaining the wonder of a novice. Stay a lifelong student.

As we move into the future, it is important to have one foot firmly planted in the past, so that we can draw upon its lessons and wisdom, while also embracing the possibilities and advancements of the present and future.

What I am trying to teach the younger generation through my podcast is exactly that: the best between the two is almost always a mix of both. This is true when you are discussing the past and the future, the East and the West, and just about any other spectrum—and much like many of my lessons, this is true both in business and in many other areas of life.

Key Takeaway

We aim to spread the message of combining the solutions of the past with the improvements of the present and future, empower and educate young people, and create a brighter and more equitable future.

25

Keep an Eye on the Future

I have always been interested in taking risks and exploring new areas for investment. Recently, I focused on innovative technologies such as AI, climate change, and space. This shift in perspective has brought great benefits to my company and the world.

One such investment was in an innovative venture called Pulse Evolution Corporation, which started its journey in the 'digital human' space with the aim of revolutionizing the way people interact with digital characters in entertainment, gaming, and other industries. I met the company's founder, John Textor, around 2018, when Pulse Evolution was traded on the US OTC and had a market capitalization of roughly $30 million. The company made headlines in 2014 when it brought Michael Jackson back to life on the stage as a hologram for the Billboard Music Awards, which was achieved using its cutting-edge technology. Eventually, Pulse Evolution renamed itself.

You may recall the viral video of a holographic Tupac performing at Coachella back in 2012. As soon as I saw that video, I knew I had to get involved with this amazing technology and company. In 2018, John, the company's founder and CEO, was trying to raise $50 million to recreate a Broadway show that would digitally resurrect the great Michael Jackson.

Patrick with good friend and business partner,
entertainment technology pioneer John Textor in 2021

The trouble was that such an endeavour would take well over two years—it would take time to secure the venue and also to create the show. I suspected at the time that John would not be able to raise the money because investors likely would not have the patience or risk tolerance for the project. Still, the underlying technology was so interesting, I wanted to find a way to participate.

The technology and the shareholders, including Tencent, Elvis Presley family estate, Michael Jackson family estate, Marilyn Monroe family estate, and the Lego family, were enough for me to know that this had the ingredients to become successful. It needed a bit of Tsangs magic. We helped to spearhead a more strategic effort, investing Tsangs Group funds, and bringing in some of our family and friends from Hong Kong, China, and

Japan. One year later, we rebranded Pulse Evolution company, buying the 'FaceBank.com' URL from Elon Musk and his team.

In September 2019, FaceBank Group completed its majority acquisition of Nexway AG, a German-listed digital solutions company with a global footprint. This acquisition gave FaceBank Group the ability to offer merchants around the world turnkey solutions for their global ecommerce needs and infrastructure. With its acquired companies and technology, FaceBank Group aims to become the world leader in the emerging digital human- and face-related industries.

During my time working with FaceBank, I had a few high-profile opportunities to bring on celebrity athletes, including Floyd Mayweather and David Beckham. We had signed an agreement with Floyd Mayweather Jr—the undefeated boxing legend, record holder of fifty consecutive wins and zero losses—on 31 July 2019. I travelled to Vegas with John Textor to produce content for his hologram and promo for the brand. All the equipment came down from Los Angeles ready to go with Scantruck. We were supposed to film one morning at a local gym where he trained. A whole team of us was waiting for him, and he didn't show up for whatever reason. There had been some disagreements within his management team.

I met David Beckham through my friend Caroline Rush, CEO of the British Fashion Council, at a luncheon she invited me to in Shanghai, pre-COVID-19, in 2018. Beckham had recently been appointed as the Global Ambassador for the British Fashion Council to promote British brands worldwide, with a focus on the Chinese market. I had the opportunity to sit opposite Beckham during lunch and discuss FaceBank and pitched the idea of creating a hologram for Beckham. He was completely open to the idea and very friendly. I met his team back in London too. However, we could not put the deal together before 2020. While the company had traction, it was essentially losing money. We saw further distribution potential and merged FuboTV (the Netflix for live sports in North America) in April 2020 with FaceBank. The combined entity was then listed on the New York Stock Exchange in October 2020.

Patrick with David Beckham at the Middle House, Shanghai in 2018

FuboTV went public on New York Stock Exchange six months later in October 2020 at a valuation of $2.5 billion. The stock was also followed by the WallStreetBets, and the company went onto a $9 billion market cap, which meant we made 300x in less than two years.

This complex deal ended up becoming the biggest and best investment we had ever made in our careers. Because of that success, we were able to re-strategize and turn Tsangs Group into the global powerhouse it is today.

Technology has the tremendous power to create value for everyone involved, and that value creation leads to freedom. This experience has also inspired me to think even bigger and make strategic investments in areas like plasma propulsion that have the potential to shape the future of humanity for centuries to come. Hence, we invested recently in a space company that designs plasma propulsion engines, based out of Texas in the US.

Despite facing challenges such as major surgery and the pandemic, I have continued to work toward these goals with passion and determination. While many people may have chosen to take it easy and focus on maintaining the status quo during these grim times, I chose to stick to my belief in the importance of hard work and striving for success. For me, it is like playing music—when you genuinely love what you are doing, you do not get tired of it, even when things get tough. This is my music and love.

Key Takeaway

Innovative technology coupled with a proactive investment style and, of course, a little bit of luck, can lead to transformative results. These results, in turn, allow for increased freedom and flexibility to focus on the endeavours that really matter.

26

The Effects of the Pandemic

It was 2.30 in the afternoon on 9 October 2020, when I experienced one of the momentous events that would impact my—and my family's—life in the midst of a raging COVID-19 pandemic.

After leaving my home in Hong Kong for London, I had intended to take advantage of the change of scenery and use the time in quarantine to think, reflect, and plan for the future. However, achieving this state of solace was far more challenging than I anticipated.

As a global citizen accustomed to near-constant travel, I found it hard to stay in one place for too long. It was only a few weeks into my strategic relaxation retreat, and I was already feeling restless.

The calendar reminder on my mobile chimed, reminding me that it was almost time to begin. I pulled out my laptop, fired up my browser, and joined the Zoom meeting.

There on the screen was a familiar sight, the balcony of the New York Stock Exchange. Behind it, the giant digital screens cast a red hue as the FuboTV logo appeared in crisp white. Eight people joined us on the screen, five of whom were men in dark suits who rang the opening bell and celebrated the start of FuboTV's public trading.

I watched silently for a moment and then slowly closed my laptop. Tsangs Group, the family office founded by my grandfather and now under my leadership, had invested in FuboTV years earlier. Now, with this IPO, it represented the single largest return we had ever generated.

It's been my vision to transform the organization into something that can impact beyond mere value creation. Something more extensive and more dynamic than what it was intended to be, a testament to my family's legacy that also plays a role in shaping the future.

The FuboTV deal represented a significant step in this direction. Not only was it a deal that I conceived and shepherded to this point, but it was also the largest and most impactful non-real estate investment we'd ever made.

It should, by all estimations, have been a moment for supreme celebration. The COVID-19 pandemic, however, made that virtually impossible. Instead, I found myself sitting in the silence of my home, immersed in the profound cognitive dissonance of the moment.

I was, at the same time, both thrilled and profoundly disappointed. We had just experienced a huge win, to be sure, but I felt like I was missing something. I've had many successes in my life, but this was, at least monetarily, the largest. I suppose that part of me always thought the next big win would be the one to make me feel satisfied. Yet here I was, feeling lost. The pandemic caused many disruptions to normal life. I imagined all the other people, especially young people, who needed a sense of direction and source of inspiration—just like I did at the time.

To that end, I started a video podcast called *Anything is Possible*, and I managed to interview my boyhood football idol, the legendary England and Liverpool winger John Barnes. As a die-hard fan of Liverpool from the age of seven, it was surreal getting to talk with him about his life, football, and work in making football a more racially equitable industry. John is a true global citizen, being of Jamaican descent and playing for England. Throughout the 1980s, he endured racial abuse on the pitch, enduring jeers, monkey noises, and even facing the despicable act of bananas being thrown at him by extreme far-right activists.

He brought awareness to racism throughout his career and after that, through speaking at conferences and events, and writing his book, *The Uncomfortable Truth About Racism*. He broke down barriers through his game. John was my hero. When I was growing up, he was the only prominent Black football player in the UK. I did not like him because he was different like me or a Black guy. I liked him because of his mesmerizing football skills on the pitch and his results. He just happened to be a person of colour. Race did not even register in my mind. Merit did.

One thing that resonated with me is that once I had grown up, and when I met him, it dawned on me that he was also facing and had faced racial prejudice throughout his life, and just like me, he was also another human being. He's an ethnic minority in that sense and was subjected to racial prejudice—just like I was when I was younger.

While he was at the top of his game, he maintained peak performance, not letting this racism and discrimination affect him. That was an inspiration to me. It showed me that even my hero had vulnerabilities and even he had to overcome similar challenges.

He's just another human being. This was a breakthrough in how I saw racism, and how we are all different but all the same.

I am fortunate and proud to be able to call him my friend now, with whom I can chat about anything. He is one of the nicest, kindest men I know and is extremely intelligent. Also, the fact I grew up watching him on TV and now I can chat to him like a normal human being, it really shows that anything is possible. This young Chinese boy from Belfast really came a long way, and the same goes for John's story also. We all have our own story to tell.

Patrick with good friend John Barnes MBE, legendary England and Liverpool football player, at Anfield football stadium in 2022

The pandemic shed light on deeper, more existential issues humanity was facing. On top of racial inequities, it highlighted the interconnectedness and fragility of our global systems and exposed the inequalities and vulnerabilities that exist within them.

Logistics, supply chain, and food security were all challenges that everyone faced during the crisis, and governments had to intervene and assist.

It also brought attention to the importance of preparedness and resilience in the face of crisis, and the need for collective action and cooperation to address global challenges.

As we continue to navigate the aftermath of the pandemic, it is crucial that we take these lessons to heart and work toward building a more sustainable, equitable, and resilient future for all. This will require addressing the root causes of these issues and finding ways to address them at a systemic level. It will also require a willingness to innovate and adapt, to embrace change and uncertainty, and to work toward a shared vision of a better future for all.

In a sense, the pandemic was a period of self-reflection for me, and it forced me to do things differently. In order to move forward and secure a bright future for myself and for society, I knew that I needed to address the pressing issues and challenges facing us head-on. Ignoring or trying to distract from these problems would not make them go away, and I knew that I had to take action to address them. This meant confronting issues such as climate change and finding ways to leverage technology to mitigate its impacts and build a more sustainable future. It also meant being proactive, rather than reacting to problems as they arise. Only by taking bold action and tackling these challenges head-on could I hope to reclaim my 'blue sky' and pave the way for a clear, bright future for all.

Key Takeaway

When so-called 'black swan' events, like the COVID-19 pandemic, hit, they can represent meaningful opportunities for growth and development.

27

Danger and Opportunity in Crisis

In the Chinese language, the word 'crisis' is composed of two characters, 危機, one representing danger or risk and the other representing opportunity or change.

In times of crisis, it is important to recognize that there are always opportunities for growth and advancement. Those who are able to see and seize these opportunities, even in the midst of danger and uncertainty, are often the ones who thrive and succeed.

This was certainly true during the pandemic, when some companies and individuals struggled to adapt, while others found new ways to thrive and reach levels of success that were previously unimaginable. The key is to stay alert and proactive, to be ready to take advantage of opportunities as they arise, and to never give up.

In addition to the opportunity for growth and advancement, crisis also brings change—and change is the only constant in life. During the pandemic, I saw firsthand how quickly things can change and how important it is to be adaptable and open to new possibilities. Even when life feels monotonous, there are always changes and developments happening in the world around us, and it is important to be aware of and responsive to these shifts.

During the pandemic, our lives were marked by constant change and uncertainty. New rules and regulations were being introduced almost daily, and we had to adapt to new ways of working, communicating, and interacting with one another. This change was exhausting, but those who were able to overcome the fatigue and continue to excel in their work and personal lives gained the most in this constantly shifting landscape.

I think back to my time at Harvard Business School, which was during COVID-19. Eduardo, a Brazilian member of my living group, played a crucial role in a memorable incident during our negotiation workshop. The first session was fairly straightforward, but the second one presented a unique challenge as it involved a team negotiation with two people against two. My team consisted of Eduardo and I, and we went against Paula and Ahmed.

The night before this critical workshop, in a rather typical fashion, I led a group of my classmates to venture into Chinatown for some karaoke fun. The evening was a mix of cultures, with a number of Chinese and non-Chinese classmates joining in. I found myself leading this diverse group, embarking on a night of continuous drinking and singing. A Chinese friend, Qian, encouraged us to keep up with the local drinking pace, which resulted in all of us—including me—getting exceptionally drunk. I barely recall how I got home that night.

Subsequently, I missed the first lesson of the morning but made sure I would participate in the negotiation workshop. I could not let my partner, Eduardo, down. At our program, missing four sessions was the limit, and I had already missed another due to a trip to Miami the weekend before. Realizing the importance of not letting my team down, I texted Eduardo, admitting to my hungover state and emphasising the need for him to lead the upcoming negotiation.

From the outset, I did not see the value in reading the cases beforehand as I saw the value of the course in the networking aspect of it rather than the content. I, thus, did not prepare for this workshop and read the homework. However, to my surprise,

Eduardo did not show up for the session and I still stank of alcohol—he had contracted COVID-19! This left me alone against the well-prepared Paula and Ahmed, who had come equipped with an extensive analysis and an Excel spreadsheet comparing the various scenarios. Despite my lack of preparation and reading the case on the fly, I leveraged my negotiation experience in real life to navigate the workshop negotiation. In the end, I advocated against striking a deal, sensing that their eagerness hinted at a disproportionately advantageous deal for them. The post-mortem analysis of the negotiation in class was eye-opening. My opponents perceived my approach as very well-prepared and hard-negotiated, unaware of my actual lack of preparation.

The key takeaway from this experience was twofold: You never know if any unforeseen circumstances arise, so one has to be able to adapt and be flexible, and more subtly, the significance of demeanour, body language, and perceived confidence in negotiations. It reinforced the idea that sometimes, in life's unanticipated situations, one must rely on innate skills and the art of perception to navigate through.

The pandemic fundamentally changed the way we live and do business, and it accelerated the adoption of new technologies in a way that was previously unimaginable. Video calls, fintech, digital health, and agriculture were just a few of the areas that saw tremendous growth and innovation during this time.

For me, the pandemic opened my eyes to the possibility of new methods of communication and collaboration, and it forced me to adapt and be creative in the way I did business. It was a challenging and transformative period, but it also presented opportunities for growth and advancement that I am grateful to have been able to seize.

Green finance is widely seen as the future of the financial industry, but the pandemic has also driven innovation and growth in other areas, such as artificial intelligence, space exploration, and blockchain. Fintech, in particular, has become mainstream, with Bitcoin becoming a household name.

It is worth noting that China has played a particularly influential role in the development of blockchain and digital currency. The country was one of the earliest adopters of these technologies and recognized the potential power and opportunity for decentralization of power that they offered. China decided to take a proactive approach and shape the future of these technologies to suit its own interests.

As we look toward the future, it is clear that digital currency will play an increasingly significant role in our lives. It will be an open and transparent system, allowing everyone to see exactly how much money is being spent, on what, and by whom. This level of transparency and accountability has the potential to bring about significant changes in the way we live and do business.

The pandemic has brought about significant changes in the global landscape, and these changes are likely to continue in the coming years. One of the most significant shifts is the increasing influence of digital currency and the decentralization of traditional financial systems. As digital currency becomes more prevalent, it will be trackable and transparent, potentially changing consumer behaviour and the way that countries do business.

In this changing environment, technologies such as artificial intelligence, electric vehicles, and ESG (Environment, Social, and Governance) will become more critical than ever before.

The rivalry between the US and China will also shape global geopolitics, and there will be shifts in biopharma and supply chains as well. Inflation and debt will also be critical issues to address.

As we move into the digital age, it is clear that we will need to embrace these changes and find ways to navigate and thrive in this new landscape. It will require adaptability, innovation, and a willingness to embrace new technologies and ways of doing things.

Key Takeaway

Danger and opportunity go hand in hand. It takes wisdom to balance both and take advantage of situations when the time is right.

28

The Future of Tsangs Group

Many entrepreneurs and founders ask me how to create a vision and if they need one. I believe it is paramount to have the vision of what you are trying to set out to do. But is it a complete prerequisite? I believe that the vision can and will change over time. Sometimes, at the beginning, you might think you will be selling orange juice. However, in the end, maybe you end up selling smoothies. So, the vision can change. But it's about finding the right combination, which includes finding a combination of the right people to help you execute your vision. The team and people are key. You have to rely on good people who can adapt and improvise. If you have the wrong people, it will result in a bad combination, and everything will fail eventually.

You have also got to have the right systems in place to make sure that you are not overspending, doing enough in marketing; you are doing enough in terms of not hiring too many people, or if you need to go and hire more people, or to do more sales, or do whatever it may be. But ultimately, the vision is important, because the founder or the CEO, or the chairperson has to make sure that the vision has to be clear. And the vision has to be there so that everyone understands where it is.

It's the job of the CEO to safeguard the vision of the company. Steve Jobs said, 'The most powerful person in the world is the storyteller. The storyteller sets the vision, values, and agenda of an entire generation that is to come.' That's the purpose. Sometimes people forget or lose focus of the purpose because they are busy executing and doing all the tasks that they have in front of them on a daily basis. Vision is really important. It is only when you have the vision of the way that the company should be run, then you then have the culture. For example, going into 2024 we collectively as a group reviewed our vision and mission. We also created new principles for the Group and to help guide the team towards those goals.

1. Life is not fair. Try your best.
2. The more you dream, the more you achieve.
3. No limitations. Be Creative. Be entrepreneurial.
4. Be flexible, adaptable, and agile.
5. 'Too much work' is never an excuse.
6. Making mistakes is fine as long as we learn and grow from it.
7. Pick up the poo. Take ownership regardless of title, position, or situation.
8. Never give up. Stay resilient and persevere.
9. Respect others. We are all equals at every level.
10. Anything is possible. There are no limits to achieving success.

I saw a quote recently saying that if Nike was to open a hotel, people would imagine very quickly, easily in their own minds, how a Nike hotel would look. It would be modern, cool, and trendy, exactly like any Nike product, store, or website. But if Hilton, the hotel brand, was going to start a sneaker brand, no one would know what it would look like. This is because Hilton does not have a brand like Nike does. Hilton is just a name that people recognize for hotels that range from economical to expensive, but there is no real added value in the Hilton brand. Nike, on the other hand, is different. It is all about the brand. I think for me, the company, the idea, the founders, the brand, the business model, the culture is all in one, and it all needs to be in sync and supported by the team in order for it to be successful.

At Tsangs Group, our vision is to continue to innovate and create value in diverse ways. We started off as farmers, moved to the UK, started Chinese restaurants, and expanded to residential and commercial real estate. In the last ten to fifteen years, our vision has been to focus on world-changing technology that can positively impact the world.

I believe that the DNA of the business is to keep moving, keep charging forward to see what the trends are, and keep changing and see how we can fit in. That is why we are agile and opportunistic. To us, the only constant is change.

I always embrace change, and our family is open to change. No task scares us; we like venturing into the unknown. I began funnelling these future-focused goals into the Group. I made new goals for the future of Tsangs Group. The pandemic forced me to change and pivot our collective responsibility and potential. Whilst many were gripped by fear, I always embraced challenging times. I saw an opportunity for bold action aimed at achieving our loftiest dreams.

Tsangs Group was founded with a strong focus on achieving positive impact through its various investments and activities in sectors such as renewables, biotech and life sciences, artificial intelligence, robotics, mobility, software, and gaming and entertainment tech.

An example of our focus is when we invested in the Ad Astra Rocket Company in March 2021. Ad Astra was founded by former NASA astronaut Franklin Chang-Díaz, who is the Guinness World Record holder of going on space missions through Space Shuttle seven times in total. Born and raised in

Costa Rica and being the first Latin American NASA astronaut to go into space, Franklin graduated with his PhD degree from MIT, where he first seeded with the initial concept of VASIMR engine. The VASIMR engine is ten times more efficient than traditional chemical rockets. It enables us to reach Mars in just ninety-five days. To the best of my knowledge, the best technology today from the market takes eight months to go to Mars. The applications of the VASIMR engine includes space station re-boost, orbital debris mitigation, satellite servicing and refuelling, space resource recovery, and fast human transport. The project is fully supported by NASA and is expected to disrupt the space engine industry. The project still has a few milestones to go before they can commence its commercialization.

Today, our commitment to impact through our company and the Tsangs Charity Foundation is reflected in our three primary value pillars: education, youth empowerment, and shaping a better future. These pillars are all united by a shared optimism that anything is possible, and that the future of humanity is bright. We believe that the ideas and individuals who can lift humanity up are already among us; they just need the right opportunities and support to achieve their dreams. In turn, we have hosted multiple internship programmes, given lectures to local schools, and have subsidised some of our staff's higher education.

Our company started with the Tsang family patriarch, a keen supporter of education for his family and the broader Hakka community he served. His humbling story of hard work, dedication, and perseverance formed the foundation of our modern family office. My great grandfather's principle, 'the power of the pen is mightier than power of the sword,' reflects a profound understanding of the transformative power of education within the context of his family's history and the societal dynamics of the Qing Dynasty.

Inspired by this ethos, my grandfather became the first in the family and village to pursue an education. This pivotal decision not only altered the course of his own life but also set in motion a ripple effect that transcended generations. The transformative impact of education reverberated throughout the family and the village, affecting the lives of 300 families and subsequently influencing the establishment of businesses, including restaurants. This enduring commitment to education, deeply embedded within the family's ethos, transcended cultural boundaries and became a guiding principle for subsequent generations. It manifested in a dedicated focus on education, which ultimately led to the establishment of a charitable foundation with a core mission of promoting and facilitating educational opportunities for others. His teachings serve as a testament to the enduring significance of education as a catalyst for individual and collective upliftment.

He proves that knowledge and learning have the power to break cycles of poverty, elevate communities, and shape brighter futures for generations to come. This is how we developed the pillars of our social initiative strategy.

That is the impact that Tsangs Group is dedicated to supporting and promoting around the world.

Key Takeaway

A clear vision for your company is paramount and crucial for success. The vision can evolve, requiring adaptability, but it serves as a guiding force for the founder or CEO to ensure clarity and alignment within the team.

29

Hong Kong Ambassadors Club

Before COVID-19, I had an agreement with the King of Private Members' Clubs in London, Robin Birley, to co-found a Chinese Business Club in London, Beijing, and New York. I had the vision that the top Chinese businesspeople and their Western counterparts would be able to interact and mingle in luxury and private space in the three power cities.

Obviously, COVID-19 came, and the world stopped for a couple of years. China also changed geopolitically, and the business between China and the other Western countries thus changed significantly. Fortunately, not starting the project saved us a lot of money because during the current geopolitical climate, this concept of a Chinese Business Club probably would not work.

Also, pre-COVID-19, since President Trump came into power, the geopolitical tensions between the US and China have been deteriorating day by day. I have many American friends, and I know Americans and Chinese share many commonalities such as working very hard and trying to make money and treating education very highly. I thought the idea of us not doing business together would affect the whole world. Here we have the two richest and most powerful nations in the world, and one wonders, wouldn't the world be a better place if we both worked together instead of fighting each other?

I spoke to many American and Chinese businesspeople and government officials during pre-COVID-19 times in an attempt to form the US-China Friendship Association, where we would, through trade and business, engage with each other and build our connections and strengthen our relationships.

This, again, did not happen due to COVID-19 and the ever-worsening relations between US and China.

You can see that my vision and efforts are always towards peace and engagement and constructive building of bridges between people and communities. There is an African proverb that says, 'If you want to go fast, go alone. If you want to go far, go together.' I believe we should always engage with each other and keep building bridges to connect us to go further. Much further.

Engaging with others also helps you learn new things and challenge your beliefs. For instance, in the summer of 2022, I spent a lot of time in southern Europe where I met a lot of Americans (who were taking advantage of the weak Euro) who asked where I was from. When I told them that I was from Hong Kong, they responded by saying that Hong Kong was great—please take note of the use of the past tense—but its greatness was thing of the past. I explained frantically that Hong Kong was still Asia's World City and the coolest city in the world. It was brushed aside.

During the pandemic, I spent almost two years away from Hong Kong. When I went back to Hong Kong in August 2022, I was in quarantine for a few days, and I was so excited to be back to see the beautiful harbour, smell the Hong Kong I know, see my family and friends, and eat my beloved dim sum and wonton noodles. However, I was shocked and saddened to see the deserted streets; the energy of the most vibrant city had been drained somehow. Shops in the busiest areas, such as Mongkok and Causeway Bay, were empty and closed. I knew I had to do something to help Hong Kong back on its feet.

I was brainstorming and exploring. This vision led to the founding of the Hong Kong Ambassadors Club ('HKAC') in 2023 by several like-minded business leaders and me. I partnered with my good friend, business partner, and mentor, who I mentioned earlier in the book, the Honourable Jeffrey Lam, GBM, GBS, JP, a member of the Legislative Council and executive council of the Hong Kong Special Administrative Government.

(From left to right) Mr King Leung, head of financial services and FinTech at InvestHK; Dr King Au, executive director of the Financial Services Development Council (FSDC); Mr Patrick Tsang, founder of HKAC; His Excellency Ricky Suhendar, consul general of Indonesia; Mr Christopher Hui, GBS, JP, secretary for Financial Services and the Treasury of the HKSAR government; His Excellency Shaikh Saoud Ali Almualla, consul general of the United Arab Emirates; Ms Salina Yan JP, permanent secretary for Financial Services & the Treasury (Financial Services) of the HKSAR government; the Hon. Jeffrey Lam, GBS, JP, founder of HKAC; and Attorney Roberto Mabalot, vice consul (Commercial) and Commercial Attaché at Philippine Trade and Investment Centre for the inauguration ceremony of Hong Kong Ambassadors Club in 2023

As a Hong Kong-based investor with operations across the globe, including Southeast Asia and the Middle East, I understood the vast untapped potential for trade and investment partnerships. Deals were waiting to be brokered, ideas to be shared, and relationships to be born. But too often barriers of language, geography, and culture prevented these opportunities from materialising.

The intention behind HKAC was to build bridges across these divides. We sought to connect companies and innovators to foster mutual understanding and prosperity. Our worldwide Chinese diaspora represented a valuable network that could be mobilised to promote Hong Kong's strengths. Envisioning to promote the brand of 'Hong Kong Inc.', the HKAC drives impactful business groups and top-level investor networks to bridge Hong Kong with strategic regions such as the Middle East, highlighting the UAE and Saudi Arabia as prime locations to connect and foster deeper relations through business and investment partnerships.

I embraced the chance to put this vision into action. My international business experience equipped me well to identify synergies and navigate nuances across borders. I brought the strategic perspective to turn good intentions into tangible initiatives that created value.

Above all, this undertaking aligned with my personal leadership ethos. Those blessed with fortune and influence must give back to society. Prosperity multiplies when shared openly rather than hoarded in isolation. By facilitating win-win collaborations, HKAC could contribute to progress.

HKAC established two primary objectives guiding our programs and operations. The first was championing Hong Kong as a destination for technology and finance. Despite negative perceptions due to its political turmoil, Hong Kong offered advantages few other cities could match. Its laissez-faire policies, robust legal system, and business expertise created the ideal environment for enterprises to thrive.

Already home to one of the world's largest financial hubs, Hong Kong also harboured the potential to become a global innovation hub. With proper coordination and promotion of its capabilities, especially in fields like biotech and renewables,

Hong Kong could attract investment and talent to cement its stature further.

HKAC's second main objective involved forging partnerships between Hong Kong, the Greater Bay Area, and many other regions globally, including the resource-rich Gulf states and Southeast Asia through bilateral trade business, investment delegations, and facilitating partnerships and collaborations between the senior leaders in the public and private sectors among the regions.

Though separated by immense distance, these regions, in fact, complemented each other remarkably well. Their synergies spanned logistics, commodities, tourism, digital services, and more.

However, businesses often needed more channels and relationships to identify and develop cooperative ventures across cultures. Here, HKAC could provide the connective tissue to fuse these clusters of expertise together and spur symbiotic growth.

Specifically, we envisioned Hong Kong's advanced professional services and digital capabilities combined with the manufacturing expertise of Greater Bay Area cities like Shenzhen. Meanwhile, the capital and natural resources of the Middle East could integrate into the supply chains and offerings of the other regions.

Our flagship activity involved organizing delegations of Hong Kong business leaders to visit strategic partner countries, particularly in the Middle East. These trips showcased Hong Kong's unique offerings while deepening our understanding of collaboration opportunities.

Delegates represented fields like renewables, robotics, food tech, banking, logistics, real estate, and technology. Their packed schedules included tours of free trade zones, meetings with top officials, networking receptions, and deal-signing ceremonies.

The first major delegation visited the UAE in June 2023, setting the tone for subsequent trips. This early success cemented HKAC's reputation as an impactful convener.

Among the tangible outcomes were cooperative frameworks around shipping logistics, food technology transfers, and smart city development. These aligned neatly with our goals of connecting Hong Kong enterprises to promising ventures abroad.

Even on our home turf, HKAC is focused on nurturing Hong Kong's next generation of companies, with particular focus on smart city solutions and food technology. Hong Kong faces challenges around liveability, sustainable growth, and resource management as its population expands. HKAC spotlights innovative startups offering technology solutions relevant to these needs.

For instance, we showcase AI-enabled traffic systems, green construction materials, automated waste management, and other urban advancement technologies. By connecting these ventures to municipal partners and investors, HKAC aims to seed smarter city infrastructure. Similarly, as food security and safety issues mount globally, Hong Kong is primed to spearhead technologies from precision aquaculture to vertical farming to ethical meat production. Local universities and entrepreneurs are already pioneering such advances.

Through showcases, policy proposals, and linking startups to pilot customers, HKAC fosters an ecosystem to support Hong Kong's food tech ambitions and export solutions worldwide.

The opportunities emerging from these initiatives soon attracted interest from major entities outside the region. Once initial Memorandums of Understanding were in place, HKAC worked to transition these relationships into full-fledged project partnerships.

Within a noticeably short time frame of twelve months, HKAC made great strides toward fulfilling our mission through targeted programs that yielded concrete outcomes.

On top of these tangible results, HKAC expanded Hong Kong's brand equity and relationships immeasurably. Our consistent presence at high-profile events worldwide put

Hong Kong innovation in the spotlight. And our facilitation of cross-border connections fostered goodwill and understanding.

By laying these foundations through our strategic initiatives, we cultivated fertile soil for ideas and partnerships to blossom. These seeds may bear fruit for years as collaborations deepen long after delegations have returned home. A true bridge builder focuses not on immediate transactions but on enduring bonds.

A proud moment for HKAC was in December 2023, leading our first delegation to COP28 in the UAE and hosting the first Hong Kong Climate Day at the China Pavilion in the Dubai Expo site. As Hong Kong has been well elevated and repositioned as the as 'Green Finance' hub for Asia, the Hong Kong Ambassadors Club joined hands with the Deeprock Group in the Blue Zone, founded by Mr Wang Shi, the founder of Vanke Group and honorary chairman of the board of directors of Vanke Group.

While the Deeprock Group, previously known as the Vanke Group, under the leadership of Mr Wang, who is also the UN Environment Goodwill Ambassador and President of WWF China, has been sponsoring the China Pavilion for the last thirteen years, this year was the first time the private sectors in Hong Kong (especially with the circles of family office leaders) were invited and curated as an official part of the China Pavilion. The Honourable Jeffrey Lam, who is also the co-founder of the Hong Kong Ambassadors Club, conducted high-level dialogue with Mr Wang as part of the negotiation agenda, clarifying and laying out a stronger role which Hong Kong could play in global green finance and roles which family offices in Hong Kong, even the Greater Bay Area (the nine cities in Guangdong Province and the two special administrative regions: Hong Kong and Macau) could lead.

On Hong Kong Climate Day, 8 December 2023, HKAC hosted a series of sessions in the Blue Zone over the themes on climate-proof technologies, innovations, and impact investment with the roles of the next generations of family offices and technology entrepreneurs. 'Made-in-Hong Kong' climate pioneers and entrepreneurs in sectors such as future food, robotics, future fashion, and future housing (clean energy and electricity) were invited.

During COP28, I had the honour to be in the presence of His Majesty King Charles III, whom I chatted with about climate issues and His Highness Sheikh Mohamed bin Zayed Al Nayhan, president of the UAE, and His Highness Sheikh Mohammed bin Rashid Al Maktoum, ruler of Dubai at the COP28 Business and Philanthropy Climate Forum. The reception was hosted by the COP28 Presidency in strategic partnership with the Sustainable Markets Initiative (SMI), attended by global heads of state and governments, business CEOs, philanthropists, and heads of NGOs. I connected with legendary investor Ray Dalio, Mariam Almheiri, minister of Climate Change and Environment of the UAE, HRH Princess Lamia Al Saud, and the US special presidential envoy for climate John Kerry, as well as personalities like Michael Bloomberg, former mayor of New York City, Leo Varadkar, (Taoiseach) prime minister of Ireland, and David Cameron, secretary of state for Foreign, Commonwealth and Development Affairs of the UK.

Patrick with His Majesty King Charles III at COP28 Business and Philanthropy Climate Forum 2023 in Dubai, United Arab Emirates

Patrick with legendary investor Ray Dalio at COP28 Business and Philanthropy Climate Forum 2023 in Dubai, United Arab Emirates

Patrick with United States Special Presidential Envoy for Climate John Kerry at COP28 Business and Philanthropy Climate Forum 2023 in Dubai, United Arab Emirates

Patrick with HRH Princess Lamia Al Saud at COP28 Business and
Philanthropy Climate Forum 2023 in Dubai, United Arab Emirates

Key Takeaway

Ideas are seeds that can be much bigger than you expected. Always
have a purpose; it will grow from a seed into a tree or plant. Share
that vision with like-minded people.

30

The Allure of the Kingdom of Saudi Arabia

Always focused on innovation and thinking forward and ahead, Tsangs Group recognized the immense potential of strengthening ties between China and the Middle East. The Kingdom of Saudi Arabia under the rule of the Crown Prince and Prime Minister of Saudi Arabia, Mohammed bin Salman Al Saud, particularly stood out for its robust economic growth, youthful population, and sweeping modernization initiatives. To capitalize on these trends, Tsangs Group pursued strategic partnerships and agreements in Saudi Arabia over the past few years. I view Saudi Arabia, how China was in the late 1990s and early 2000s, at the beginning of major growth and full of opportunities and upcoming new cities to be constructed.

With roots in Hong Kong, Tsangs Group maintains a worldwide outlook in its investments and operations. We invest across sectors including technology, healthcare, entertainment, and finance on multiple continents. This global perspective allows us to identify promising cross-border opportunities.

Given its rising economic influence and central position along the Belt and Road Initiative, Saudi Arabia emerged as a prime location for expanding Tsangs Group's footprint.

Its bold reform agenda to diversify trade and infrastructure made Saudi an especially compelling partner. Collaborating with key Saudi entities would offer footholds into the broader region's development.

In 2023, Tsangs Group entered into strategic joint ventures with Hong Kong-based A-Grade Energy Limited and Rice Robotics Limited to pursue smart city projects in the Middle East. A-Grade brings expertise in solar energy, energy storage systems, and e-mobility solutions, including developing electric vehicle charging stations and related technologies. Meanwhile, Rice Robotics offers innovative capabilities in delivery, cleaning, and security robots ideal for sustainable cities. Under the partnership, Tsangs Group provides capital and advisory support to aid Rice Robotics expansion into Middle Eastern markets beyond its Hong Kong base.

These joint ventures demonstrate Tsangs Group's model of synergistic collaboration between Hong Kong enterprises and international partners. Our worldwide network and investment experience facilitates such cross-border relationships.

In addition to direct partnerships, Tsangs Group utilized multilateral platforms like the Belt and Road Initiative from China to accelerate entry into Middle Eastern markets. For example, we participated in prominent events like the China-Arab States Investment Symposium to showcase our technologies. Such engagements build Tsangs' brand recognition and credibility among critical regional stakeholders. They also foster relationships with political and business leaders to ease market access.

This multi-pronged strategy helps Tsangs Group leverage existing channels on our route to the Middle East. The Memorandum of Understanding signed by Tsangs Group in September 2022 with Saudi Arabia's Ministry of Investment was a major milestone during the tenth Arab-China Business Conference.

Patrick and HE Khalid Al-Falih, Minister of Investment for the Kingdom of Saudi Arabia, formalize an agreement at the tenth Arab-China Business Conference to enhance cultural collaboration and bolster business expansion in Saudi Arabia in 2023

The MoU expressed shared interest in promoting bilateral trade and cultural exchange between the Kingdom of Saudi Arabia and Hong Kong. It highlighted Tsangs Group's role in developing cooperation around technology, sustainability, smart cities, and related areas. This agreement marked a key step in solidifying Tsangs Group's involvement in helping Saudi Arabia achieve its Vision 2030 goals. It reinforced our commitment to playing a constructive role in Saudi's economic and social progress.

The MoU signing took place in the broader context of deepening commercial ties between China and the Arab world. China has become the top trade partner for numerous Middle Eastern countries. Meanwhile, Chinese firms are actively participating in strategic projects across the region. We also aim to engage further with regional bodies like the Gulf Cooperation Council that facilitate integration. This will allow Tsangs Group to share insights from China's growth experience at an institutional level to inform policy making. We also signed a MoU in collaboration with Hong Kong Ambassadors Club (HKAC) and the ROSHN Group, Saudi Arabia's first real estate developer and PIF-owned giga project. This agreement represents a significant step towards enhancing collaboration opportunities between the two parties in the field of technological investments.

Aligning with Saudi's own priorities, Tsangs Group hopes to contribute expertise and technologies to assist smart city development in major hubs like Riyadh and NEOM. Our portfolio of solutions in energy, transportation, robotics, and more are well-suited to Saudi's sustainability objectives. Tsangs Group's focus on Saudi Arabia stems from our recognition of its enormous economic promise and friendly business climate. We foresee Saudi becoming an important nexus of global capital and trade flows based on current trends.

Under policies like Vision 2030, Saudi has prioritized diversifying its economy beyond oil and gas. The Kingdom has already attracted over $100 billion in international investment to develop future growth sectors like tourism, renewables, mining, and finance.

All of this activity is powered by the ambitions of Saudi Arabia's young, digitally savvy population. Two-thirds of Saudis are under thirty-five years old, eager to engage with the world and hungry for jobs. Tsangs Group intends to participate in fulfilling their economic potential.

Overall, Saudi Arabia is poised to emerge as a dynamic hub bridging Asia, Africa, and Europe. With its pro-business reforms and openness to international partners, the opportunities for sustainable growth are plentiful. Tsangs Group looks forward to contributing knowledge, technology, and investment to aid this process.

In the Arabian Peninsula's business culture, similar to Chinese culture, personal relationships and trust hold paramount importance. Nothing happens overnight and it takes a long time and a lot of patience to build trust. This business culture is quite different to the Western way of doing business, where parties do not necessarily have to meet in person and the terms of the deal are more important. Understanding and adapting to these subtleties conveys respect while building rapport. With a long view perspective, Tsangs Group aims to forge sincere bonds with partners at all levels to enable mutually beneficial collaboration. Given the vast possibilities in Saudi Arabia and the wider Middle East, Tsangs Group is exploring potential roles in additional sectors as bilateral relations deepen. Prospects span logistics, biotech, and more.

Collaboration will remain fundamental to Tsangs Group's approach in the region. We actively seek local partners for joint ventures that combine our international expertise with intimate market knowledge. Mutual exchange of ideas, resources, and capabilities unlocks synergy.

In a very short time, Tsangs Group has fostered investment partnerships, high-level agreements, and burgeoning goodwill in Saudi Arabia specifically and the Arab world generally. This is only the prelude to an even more fruitful era ahead.

The promise of contributing to Saudi's Vision 2030, bridging Asian and Middle Eastern markets and incubating technologies that benefit humanity motivates Tsangs Group's initiatives in the region. We are eager to play a constructive role in this new world being born.

Key Takeaway

Young global leaders aiming to expand into the dynamic business landscape of Saudi Arabia should prioritize building long-term relationships and trust, understanding cultural nuances and traditions. Remember to adapt, grow, and have patience; building relationships takes time.

31

Cockroaches Don't Die So Easily

In October 2022, I had the opportunity to join a team led by Sir Richard Branson, the fittest seventy-two-year-old I have ever encountered, for the Strive Challenge trek up Mount Kenya. For those of you who might not be aware, Mount Kenya is the highest mountain in Kenya and the second highest in Africa, reaching a height of 17,057 feet (5,199 metres).

Patrick with Sir Richard Branson at the summit of Mount Kenya,
participating in the Strive Challenge with Big Change in October 2022

The mountain is considered a challenging trek, with several different routes to the summit, including the challenging technical climbing route to the main peaks. The trek up Mount Kenya takes several days and involves climbing steep rocky terrain, crossing glaciers, and dealing with unpredictable weather conditions. The altitude also presents a significant challenge, with climbers often experiencing symptoms of altitude sickness.

This challenge brought together entrepreneurs, thought leaders, and philanthropists to discuss prominent issues about education and appreciate the beauty of nature.

The Strive Challenge, founded by Sir Richard Branson's son, Sam, and his cousin, Noah, in 2012, is a series of endurance events designed to raise awareness and funds for charitable causes.

The events typically involve a gruelling multi-day trek through challenging terrain. Participants raise money for Big Change, an education-centric organization that focuses on supporting young people, regardless of their background or circumstances, to thrive in life, not just exams.

The organization's mission is to support and promote innovative and effective solutions to some of the world's most pressing social and environmental challenges.

The charity supports a range of projects and initiatives, including those related to education, environment, and health. The charity also focuses on promoting and supporting young leaders who are working to make a positive impact in their communities and around the world.

This part of the challenge was especially close to my heart, as it focused on innovative approaches to education. We engaged in deep discussions about disrupting traditional education systems and brainstorming actionable strategies to foster learning environments that cater to diverse needs and modern realities.

This challenge was not just about physical endurance but also about intellectual and emotional resilience. It was a platform where thoughts on education reform transformed into commitments and plans. The collective wisdom and dedication of this group reinforced my conviction that collaborative efforts can bring about significant changes in education. This experience was a testament to the power of uniting visionaries from various fields to address complex global issues.

Richard was also remarkably humble and down to earth given his success. He credited his team and family for their support every step of the way. He emphasized that real change requires people from all walks of life working together. No single leader can tackle global challenges alone. His sincerity and lack of ego were refreshing.

Most inspiring was the joy Richard still took in trying new things and pushing his limits. Trekking up Mount Kenya in his seventies, he retained a youthful sense of adventure. He encouraged the rest of us that age should not stop us from pursuing our passions and living boldly. I took that to heart as I continued my own unconventional entrepreneurial path in middle age.

I constantly challenge myself by trying new things outside my comfort zone. For example, I have had two hip surgeries in recent years. After the second surgery, I wanted to test my resilience, so I signed up for a charity challenge climbing Mount Kenya in Africa, one of the toughest peaks to summit.

I trained extensively in the gym to build my stamina and keep my body weight low leading up to the climb. However, due to my busy schedule, I was only able to do one real training climb beforehand in the indoor ski slope at the Mall of the Emirates in Dubai, with Tom Hudson—my good friend from the UK who has been living in the Middle East for fifteen years and also has participated in several Strive challenges. Climbing the indoor ski slope ended up being even harder than the actual ascent up Mount Kenya! We got there at 6 a.m. before other skiers came, and we walked up and down the slope over ten times.

This practice round actually made me dread the actual climb more, and I was not sure what was waiting for me as I was set to arrive in Kenya. The practice was, in some ways, tougher compared to the actual terrain in the actual climb. The five-day climb up Mount Kenya was gruelling, especially on the second day when it rained heavily consecutively for six to eight hours. It even started hailing. During the walk, when we were active, we did not feel cold. After we reached the camp to rest for the second night, I was drenched from the heavy rain, soaked to the bones and my spare clothes were not with me. I was in my cold gear for hours until the porters came with my dry clothes. During that time, my core temperature had dropped so low that I was trembling and could not do much. Eating and drinking did not help much. The only thing that was helping was singing along with Sam Branson and his trusted guitar to old 80s and 90s hits! Also, at Mount Kenya, no campfires were allowed to prevent any chance of fires spreading across the terrain. From then on until the end, every night, my body would go to such a low temperature that I was not able to function properly and because of that, every night I could not sleep properly and did not get the rest needed to meet the physical demands of the hike.

I had to dig deep mentally to conjure the energy and physical requirements to get through the day. It was quite grim, but the thought of turning back never crossed my mind and giving up was never an option for me.

I pushed through the tough conditions and was able to make it to the summit along with most of the other climbers. Four out of the twenty-four participants did not make it to the top. After getting to the top, several participants, including Richard Branson himself, commented they were surprised I persevered given how miserable I looked on some days and thought that I would be one of the first to give up and return to base camp.

I told Richard and the rest that I had been looked down on all my life. I told them that Hong Kong and Chinese people are like cockroaches, they do not die so easily. There was no way I would not make it to the top unless something physically inhibited me, like my leg breaking. Perhaps even then, I would crawl my way to the top. My mental strength would get me through this. Somehow, since a young child, I have the ability to laser focus on something that I want or need to do, and get it done, no matter how bad I feel or how much I dislike the activity. This exemplifies my 'cockroach spirit'—the resilience to survive under any conditions.

As we made our way down from the summit, we were struck by the stark changes that had occurred due to climate change. Richard, who had previously climbed the same glacier over a decade ago when it was entirely covered in snow and our guide Paul, who grew up there, remarked that the entire landscape had transformed. The snow and ice had melted significantly, revealing a landscape of mud and stones, a dramatic departure from the icy terrain he had encountered in the past. This shift in the environment was attributed to the effects of climate change, with the group noting that the warmer temperatures made the descent surprisingly comfortable despite their initial expectation of freezing conditions.

The impact of climate change on the glacier was profound, altering the once challenging climb into a different, albeit still demanding, experience. The members found themselves navigating through mountains of mud and stones, with minimal ice remaining on the slopes.

Ultimately, the trip was a meeting of twenty-four minds from all places, backgrounds, cultures, and industries. Having endured this experience together, we were able to bond in such a way that the colour of our skin had no presence or value, it was about the individual stories and hardships during the hike that mended us all together. Our simple goal was to do it together as a team, there was no racial divide. We are all equal against Mother Nature. Obviously, we had a physical common goal of reaching the summit, but our main objective was to talk about education and how the Big Change would help us transform this. It was tough physically and mentally, and we motivated and urged each other on. We talked about other issues, such as climate change, entrepreneurship, and climbing mountains. I learnt from Richard Branson about biohacking and supplements, and his daily routine in Necker and his outlook on life. Actually, I learnt from everyone on the trip. In the wild, there is no hierarchy. We are all human and we have to survive. The climbing of the summit was no mean feat, but doing it together as a team made the job much easier and happier. It was such a joy to complete the physical task with camaraderie. It was here that I realized the profound impact of collective action and the importance of nurturing a 'change-making' spirit in the realm of education and beyond.

In essence, the story captures the physical and emotional challenges of the group's descent from the glacier, while also highlighting the visible effects of climate change on the environment, serving as a powerful testament to the urgency of addressing these issues. However, I also learned that a lack of cultural understanding can often be a barrier to large-scale collaboration on this issue. It is important for us to work toward bridging this gap and finding ways to come together to address the challenges facing our planet.

I have learned this lesson through my own journey, and at the age of forty-eight (at the time of writing), I still have much more that I want to accomplish.

Key Takeaway

The Strive Challenge trek up Mount Kenya in October 2022 was a physically demanding but transformative experience that reinforced the importance of sustainability and the need for collaboration and cultural understanding in addressing urgent issues to humanity.

32

The Bridge Beyond Borders

I have always believed in engagement and connection. I am a big believer in face-to-face meetings and relationships. I believe we are all the same deep down inside and human connection cannot be replaced. One thing that human beings have done well over the centuries is build communities, which have helped us survive and flourish and have helped us mould our own identities. Community and identity building has resulted in the culture being built up and evolving over time.

I co-founded Blue Sky Scaling Limited, a technology business scaling platform for technology ventures in high-growth industries from all over the world to scale up to economically vibrant regions such as the Greater Bay Area, Middle East, and Southeast Asia with Hong Kong as the new innovation technology regional headquarters and R&D hub.

The name 'Blue Sky', a restaurant named in tribute to my grandfather, encapsulates a legacy of optimism and a commitment to businesses with promising prospects. The term 'blue sky' symbolizes limitless opportunities, reflecting the restaurant's dedication to fostering growth and success.

The primary mission is to support companies in their early growth stages or critical inflection points, guiding them to scale up operations effectively. This involves developing new business opportunities globally, with a focus on regions like the Middle East. Targeting companies beyond the MVP phase with established revenue streams, Blue Sky Scaling aims to facilitate their next growth milestone by diversifying distribution channels, broadening geographic reach, enhancing production capacity, and implementing strategic growth initiatives. The approach seeks to propel these businesses into their next developmental phase, building upon existing foundations while exploring new avenues for expansion and profitability.

The Blue Sky Scaling focuses on seven sectors including renewable energy, bio-tech and life sciences, artificial intelligence, robotics, mobility, software, and gaming and entertainment tech.

Blue Sky Scaling is a catalyst for connection and can be applied to anywhere in the world and to anyone in the world. It has roots in Hong Kong but launchpads to the rest of the world and beyond.

We are also in the process of launching Asia's first digital carbon registry EcoConsortium Hong Kong Limited. All carbon credits created need to go through audit. EcoConsortium Hong Kong is replacing traditional auditors (e.g. EY, KPMG) to automate the carbon credit audit process. We charge per carbon credit produced. After auditing, carbon credits are channelled to one of the four existing 'standard bodies' to get certified, and then they are traded in open markets (e.g. exchanges).

This will also connect Hong Kong to other Asian countries and other countries around the world for carbon credit trading. Everyone and everything are all connected.

Things are cyclical and linear at the same time. Things happen for the first time but also history repeats itself. Our family has been in Lai Chi Wo village for fourteen generations as Hakka farmers. Our ancestors built the bridge to Hong Kong when they immigrated from Guangdong province centuries ago and settled in our village today. Our fate dramatically changed when my grandfather immigrated from Hong Kong to the UK in the

1950s, building another bridge to a different continent on the other side of the world and connecting our community in Hong Kong to the UK.

Patrick visiting Lai Chi Wo in 2020, his ancestral village, now honoured as a UNESCO World Heritage Site

I was then born in the UK, but my family's cultural roots were deeply planted in Hong Kong. Interestingly, I was a stranger in both places but also understood both cultures and languages very well and lived in both places for half of my life each.

Influenced by my father, my lifelong dream was to 'move back' to Hong Kong.

I moved to Hong Kong after graduation as planned and I fulfilled and realized my dream, but after moving back, it was not the dream that I had. It was very different.

After moving back to Hong Kong, my identity and culture evolved, and I had more of a sense of belonging in Hong Kong.

It was not a light bulb moment but over time, I transitioned from identifying as a Hongkonger or British or Chinese or Irish to embracing being a global citizen. I am all of them and none of them at the same time. I am just an ordinary global citizen.

Which brings us to the question: What is a global citizen?

In the modern digital world and with the ease and convenience of flying and travelling and getting residence or citizenship, it has become much easier to move to different cities to live and work compared to my father or grandfather's time. I do not have one definition that fits all. A global citizen is a citizen of the world, whose parents may be of different cultures or religions, may live in cities they were not born in, and may speak multiple languages. It can be any of the above and more, but we are connected because we are all human and not only have differences but a lot of similarities.

I love living as a global citizen. The best part of it is the food! I can eat Chinese food, Italian food, French pastries, and Japanese sushi. Generations ago, one would only be eating the food in their own culture. Now, we have more choice and more exposure to other cultures and food. Now, we are fortunate to be able to have such varied choices, which gives us so much joy and happiness. The importance of connecting with others beyond geographical and cultural boundaries is essential to understand each other more. This understanding will help facilitate world peace and help us solve the planet's common problems together.

I have managed to live my life as a global citizen. I also work and manage my career as a global citizen. I believe I have added and created value in business due to the fact that I am a global citizen. I love promoting it and I love doing so through action.

Our mission in the family office now is to invest into technology, seeing as it has a positive impact that makes the world a better place, which is why we put emphasis on sustainability, climate change, and its global impact.

Not only do we connect with other people, but we have also gone beyond that. We have even gone beyond the boundaries of what we thought was impossible when we invested in a space technology company called Ad Astra in the US during COVID-19, as an extension of global endeavours.

The bridge is now beyond borders and is even reaching outer space!

As Bruce Lee keeps saying, we should not be bound by traditions and have no limitations. We should reject traditional notions of identity based on nationality or geography. We will use Hong Kong as a launch pad for global engagement via our various initiatives. Our vision is for transcending earthly limits and even exploring outer space.

The bridge has gone beyond what we thought it would, which reinforces the idea that the sky is certainly not the limit; there are boundless opportunities for connection and exploration.

Key Takeaway

I encourage you to form your own identity and connections in a global context. They say the sky's the limit. The blue sky is not the limit, as there is outer space and beyond. There are no limits.

Conclusion

The Global Citizen

Throughout my life and career journey, I have learned a variety of valuable lessons that have helped shape me into the person I am today. From my family and mentors, I learned resilience and strength, and in school, I learned how to use strategy and adaptability to succeed. As my integrity developed under pressure, I learned the importance of finding a balance between my family and myself, and how to listen to my intuition to discover my purpose and pursue my dreams.

In my career, I found my niche in bridging the East and West and embraced my differences as a source of strength. I stopped letting discrimination hold me back and instead saw myself through a lens of truth, recognizing that my unique qualities were a superpower rather than a hindrance. Throughout all these experiences, I have stayed true to my values and stood for equality. Together, we have explored my journey from my timid beginnings to my current daring pursuits of the new blue sky of the future. I believed in it even in the face of countless challenges. I also applied my core values to my business, ensuring that we stuck to and upheld the values we believe in every day we are in operation.

During the COVID-19 pandemic, I found a new balance between the past and the future and used my experiences to help new technology and entrepreneurs work toward a better future.

My time at home after the hip surgery brought the world into a new light, and my understanding of the importance of solving humanity's biggest problems—such as climate change and inequality—was heightened even more, moving up in my list of priorities as an evolving leader. I found art and music through piano—I started learning at the age of forty-four as my mother had rejected my request when I was seven years old and I'd asked if I could learn at school—and in it, I found the importance of mental health and bettering oneself on a holistic basis.

Looking back on my life, I am amazed at how far I have come. That scared, bullied boy who was born in Northern Ireland, who spoke no English, could hardly fathom the journey that lay ahead. There were many times I felt lost and afraid. But my family and mentors kept me going with their love and wisdom. I am so grateful for the village and the culture and teachings that raised me. I am now bringing the wisdom and experience of my past forward into the present to help new technology and entrepreneurs save the world of tomorrow.

At Tsangs Group, we are investing in positive value sectors that promote sustainability and global equality, rather than negative-value industries such as weapons and drugs. While these goals may seem ambitious, I believe that anything is possible with determination and hard work. The pandemic also taught me the importance of mental health and personal growth, and I am now using this wisdom to help others achieve their own potential.

On 25 May 2023, I experienced the profound loss of my beloved grandfather, who had a remarkable life journey reaching the age of ninety-four. In the final months of his life, I prioritized spending as much time with him as possible, cherishing each moment. The night before he passed away, I stayed close to him, sleeping on the seats next to him in the hospital. This allowed me to be by his side during his final hours, engaging in meaningful conversations throughout the night until he took his last breath.

His absence in my life is deeply felt, yet there is solace in knowing that I was there with him until his final moments. The wisdom he imparted during his lifetime, characterised by his practical approach to life, his extraordinary resilience, and his unwavering focus on moving forward, continues to be a source of daily inspiration and guidance for me.

Patrick with his grandfather, Tsang Kee Yau, at the Tsangs Group Headquarters in Hong Kong, 2022

My journey to where I am today has been a long and transformative one, surpassing the wildest dreams of my younger self in Belfast. Yet, in many ways, it feels as though my journey is just beginning. One of the most memorable moments was having the opportunity to take my grandfather to our office in Hong Kong. The pride and encouragement evident in his expression was profoundly moving, as he saw firsthand the progress and success we had achieved as a team. My grandfather, a man who usually conserved his words, offered me a simple yet powerful piece of advice: 'keep going'. Those two words had a profound impact on me, infusing me with a renewed sense of energy, motivation, and encouragement. They inspired me to continue on my path of creativity and innovation with even greater zeal.

To receive such a blessing from my grandfather is the truest form of success to me, a guiding light that continues to lead me forward.

Key Takeaway

We are all very different, yet we are all the same. Keep going. Anything is possible.

Your Turn

In order to achieve success, it is important to embrace the principles of integrity, betterment, and empathy. These values are not just my personal philosophy, but rather universal truths that can guide you toward success in your career and life.

To build your integrity, it is crucial to be honest and pure in your actions, even in the face of challenges and struggles. In addition, it is important to continuously strive to improve yourself, your business, and your surroundings for your own benefit as well as that of others and future generations.

Empathy is also crucial in this journey. It is not productive to solely focus on your own interests and ignore the impact your actions have on others. We all share this planet and must work together to make it a better place. It is important to identify your values and work toward achieving them with empathy in mind.

While the internet has made it easier for anyone to become an entrepreneur, it has also lowered the barrier to entry for others. This means that there are many businesses competing for success, making it more challenging to truly stand out. To succeed in today's business climate, it is essential to have a strong work ethic, good timing, and above all, a strong character. Remember the lessons learned and they will help guide you toward achieving your dreams.

To succeed in business, you need to stand out in some way. One way to do this is by being the first to enter a market or offering a unique product or service. Another way is by being the best at what you do, through excellent quality or customer service. Alternatively, you can differentiate yourself by approaching your industry in a unique way.

To succeed in business, you need to be either:

1. First,
2. Best, or
3. Different.

I have always been different from my peers and friends, and this difference was seen or felt to be my weakness but has become my greatest strength. Seeing from a different lens or perspective and changing your mindset will turn any negative into a positive. My grandfather, who founded Blue Sky, was also able to find success by being a mix of all three strategies—being first, being the best, and being different. In my own business endeavours, I continue to embrace my uniqueness and invest in areas that others may overlook.

It is important to note that being different is not a backup plan or a last resort. In fact, it can often be the most effective way to find success. Just look at Facebook as an example. They were preceded by MySpace and a host of other options. However, Facebook became the standard-bearer of the sector by being the first to offer two things: a relatively exclusive closed network based on shared identity and a tightly curated experience. This differentiated approach helped it become the standard-bearer in the sector.

The closed network feature was a key factor in Facebook's early success. By requiring users to have a university email address to create an account, Facebook was able to connect students at a single university and foster deeper engagement through shared experiences and environments. This helped it stand out from other social media platforms like MySpace.

In addition to the closed network, Facebook's curated experience also contributed to its growth. By standardizing profiles to a large degree, Facebook was able to create a relatively seamless experience that encouraged users to engage with each other in similar ways.

While it can be advantageous to be the first to create a new product or service, it is also possible to find success by improving upon existing ideas. X (formally Twitter), for example, built upon the concept of microblogging and turned it into a platform for sharing news and updates in real time.

It is important to keep evolving and adapting in order to sustain success over the long term. Companies like Nintendo and Amazon have demonstrated this by diversifying their offerings and expanding beyond their original products or services. Staying stuck in your ways can limit growth, while a willingness to change and adapt can help you continue to thrive. Remember, change is the only constant, and the key to sustained success.

Key Takeaway

To succeed in business, it is important to embrace integrity, betterment, and empathy as values, and to differentiate oneself through being the first to enter a market, being the best at what you do, offering a unique product or service, or approaching your industry in a unique way.

Top Seven Traits of an
Effective Leader

It is not easy to summarize one's life, but I find it helpful to have a list of tenets or tips to carry with me after finishing a journey, like the book you have just completed. Therefore, I share with you the top seven traits I think are necessary to be an effective leader.

1. **Communication**
    Communication is one of the easiest and fastest ways to build influence and leadership. Talk, but also actively listen, invite others to collaborate, and give opportunities to your employees to pitch ideas and suggestions. Giving employees a chance to share their ideas gives them confidence and makes them feel seen and heard.
2. **Honesty/Transparency**
    Build trust and honesty with your team and stakeholders by regularly communicating, team building, and growing personal connections in a straightforward and direct manner.
3. **Ownership and responsibility**
    A strong sense of ownership and responsibility as demonstrated by the 'pick up the poo' analogy is a must for leaders. Your self-awareness about your actions and how you show up is a vital trait everyone needs to develop and nurture regardless of age or position. Once

you stop trying to control your circumstances or as my dad said, 'Let the car control you,' you open yourself up to countless possibilities.

4. **Effectiveness**

   Being busy is one thing, but getting the important things done right in the right time is what counts. One needs to work smarter and not necessarily harder. As Peter Drucker said, 'Management is doing things right; leadership is doing the right things.' I have always been results driven and oriented. You can only measure results by effectiveness. One has to focus, plan, and execute— both in business and in life.

5. **Be a student of life**

   I am an avid student of life. I am always self-reflecting, expanding my mind, learning to do things better and faster, pushing myself and everyone around me to grow, and supporting my team's evolution. As an investor, I help entrepreneurs with their ideas to change the world to make it a better place.

6. **Empathy**

   Be one with your team. Show that you have genuine care and concern for them. Your employees will realize that you care about their feelings and their personal situation. As much as you can step back and scale your business and goals, number one is always taking care of the people that work for your organization and represent your brand. They will fight for you which is much needed to win a war.

7. **Purpose**

   Remind yourself of who you are, your values, what is important to you, and how you can contribute to the world. Engage your staff, partners, and audience with this mission and vision for what you want to achieve. Having a purpose will keep you motivated and hungry for success. As my father would always say, 'Life is like a show.'

If I could leave you with one motto to carry forward, one sentence from this book to remember above all the rest, it would be this:

'Learn as if it is your first day, live
as if it is your last day.'
I have told you my story.
Now, it is your turn.
Get out there and bring your special talents to the world,
whatever they are.

Build a beautiful bridge of your own design that will lead you
and all of humanity to your own new blue sky.

And do not forget: **Anything is possible!**

Acknowledgments

Anything is Possible. That has been my life philosophy. I have always wanted to write a book. Finally, it is here. Writing properly since 2018 has taken six years to get it to print.

It is not a memoir, motivation, or self-help book, but a combination of everything I believe in and my story to share with you, and you can learn something new or interesting. Only positive vibes, even if we go through tough times.

I have always gone through life against the odds, and I always triumph, maybe not how I imagined or hoped, but at least I tried my best.

I could not have done this without my partner in crime for the book and good friend and colleague, Selena Sandhu, who has been with me since the beginning of the idea. I went to Vancouver to see her and asked her to come on board, and luckily, she agreed to help me with the book. Now, she is also the PR and Marketing Director of our family office, Tsangs Group.

We spent hours and endless nights talking, discussing, plotting, and planning in person and online. This could not have been done without her.

Thank you to my colleagues in the Group, who allowed me the freedom and time to dedicate to the book.

I thank all the contributors for the forewords for their inspiration and guidance in life.

I am forever grateful and thankful to my parents for raising me and my siblings. Thank you for your hard work and sacrifice to allow me to have the platform to do my work.

Thank you to my grandfather, who started the journey and inspired many of us, especially myself. I am hoping we can carry on the good work at the family office to invest in global opportunities to make a positive impact and create a better world.

Lastly, I hope it inspires the young generation, including my own kids, to become the best version of themselves and make the world a better place.

There is nothing you cannot do. Anything is Possible.